THE ILLUSTRATED ENCYCLOPEDIA OF
OUTER SPACE

AN
A TO Z
GUIDE TO
FACTS AND
FIGURES

FOR YOUNG READERS

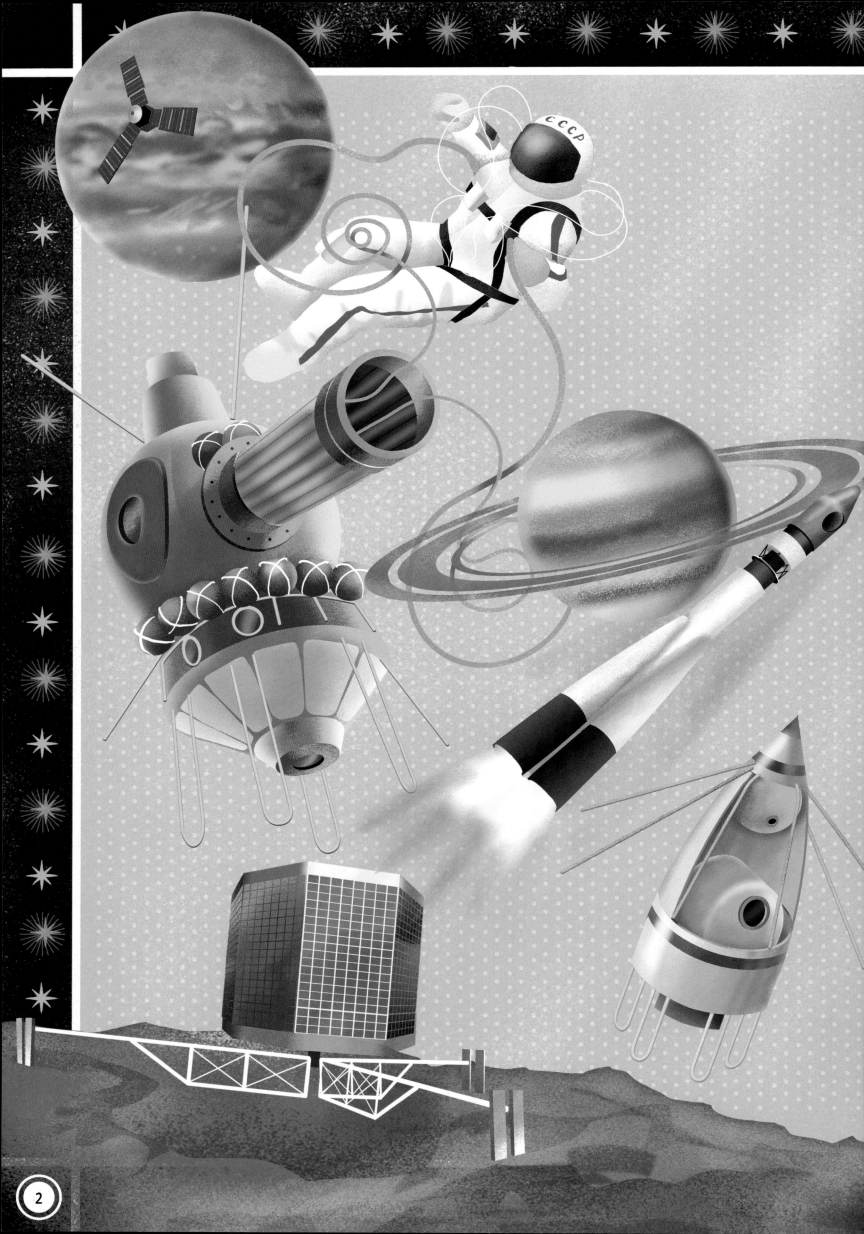

This book was written by
**Emanuela Pagliari
and Diego Mattarelli**
and was illustrated by
Annalisa Beghelli

CONTENTS

Man has always looked up into the sky: first trying to understand what those bright dots that lit up the nights were and then wishing to push beyond them, to touch the Moon! Traveling in space is a dream for many people that few ever achieve! This does not, however, prevent us from traveling with our imagination and imaging distant worlds!

The 1900s were a century filled with great achievements: man placed his foot on the Moon, space probes explored the Solar System and powerful telescopes went beyond the imaginable, sending us beautiful images of far off galaxies!
Actually, really far off! But how far?

Distances in space are enormous and cannot be measured using feet or miles. This is why astronomers invented new units of measurement. Within the Solar System, consisting of the Sun, the Earth and the seven other planets that surround us, we use the astronomical unit (AU) which is defined as the average distance between our planet and the Sun. This is equal to about 93 million miles (149 597 870 700 kilometers).

What about the most distant stars and objects that are outside the Solar System?
For these, we use the light year, that is, the distance traveled by light in a year.
Light travels at a speed of almost 185,000 mps (300,000 km/s) and, therefore, in a year it covers more than 5.88 trillion miles (9,460 trillion kilometers).

Man has also learned to live in space: on space stations like Skylab, MIR and, in recent years, on the International Space Station, astronauts are able to spend many months. To do all of this, however, we had to invent new technologies that allowed us to build rockets and space suits, but also to invent objects that we use in everyday life. Digital thermometers, cell phones, satellite navigators, the material used to make firefighter suits and sunglasses lenses that protect our eyes from ultraviolet radiation are just some of the inventions created for space and then used by everyone!

Exploring space, therefore, has not only opened up the path to new scientific discoveries, but has also helped to make our life on Earth easier!

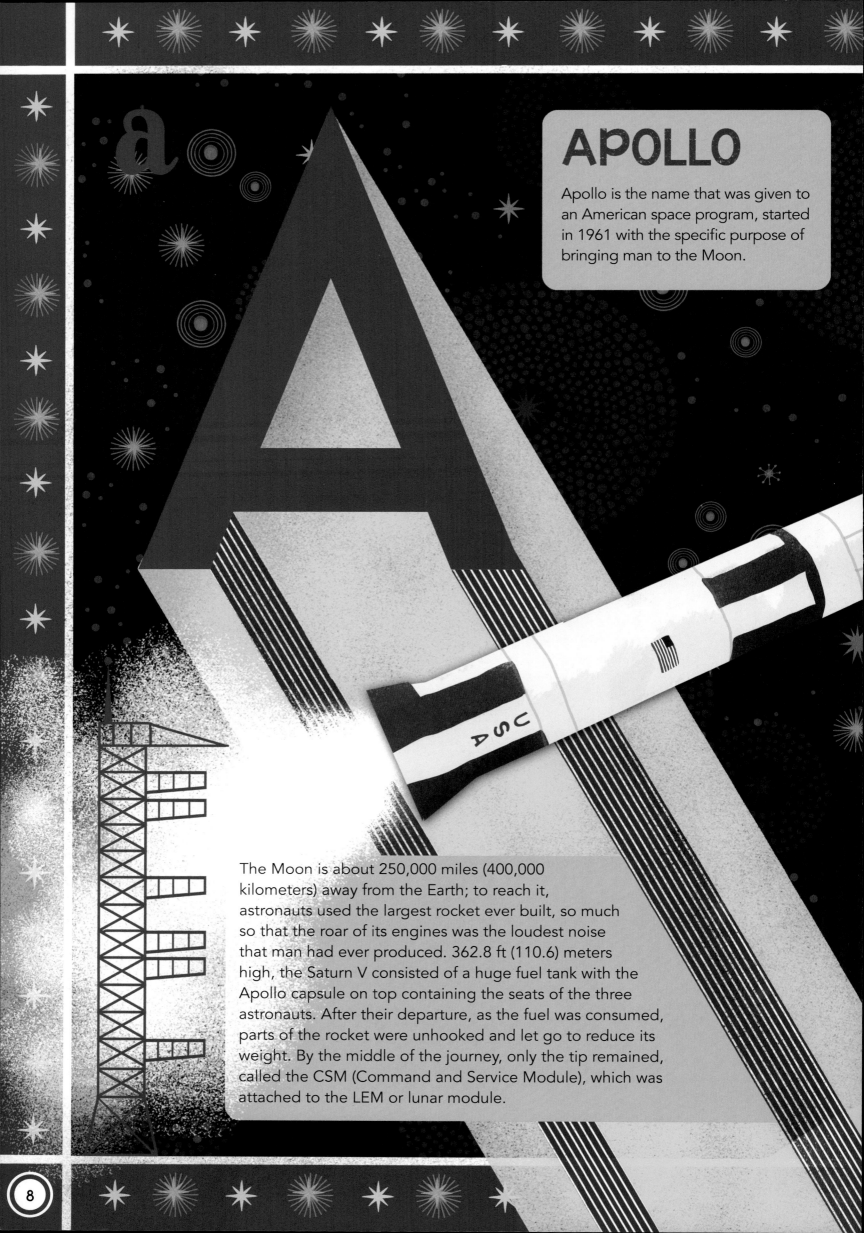

APOLLO

Apollo is the name that was given to an American space program, started in 1961 with the specific purpose of bringing man to the Moon.

The Moon is about 250,000 miles (400,000 kilometers) away from the Earth; to reach it, astronauts used the largest rocket ever built, so much so that the roar of its engines was the loudest noise that man had ever produced. 362.8 ft (110.6) meters high, the Saturn V consisted of a huge fuel tank with the Apollo capsule on top containing the seats of the three astronauts. After their departure, as the fuel was consumed, parts of the rocket were unhooked and let go to reduce its weight. By the middle of the journey, only the tip remained, called the CSM (Command and Service Module), which was attached to the LEM or lunar module.

There were a total of seventeen Apollo missions, but the first to arrive on the Moon was Apollo 11: on July 20, 1969, after a four-day trip, astronauts Neil Armstrong and Edwin "Buzz" Aldrin were the first human beings to walk on the lunar soil, while Michael Collins, the third member of the crew, was waiting for them in orbit around the Moon.

After Apollo 11, another five missions were successfully completed and only twelve men, therefore, have had the privilege of leaving their footprints on lunar soil. The astronauts of a future mission will find them again because there is no atmosphere on the Moon and therefore there are no winds and rains that can erase them.

The Moon takes 27 days to rotate fully and, at the same time, makes a complete rotation around our planet. From the Earth, therefore, you can always see only one side of our satellite. Thanks to the lunar missions, both with and without crew, it has been possible to observe and photograph even the hidden face of the Moon.

As the Moon is smaller than the Earth, it has a force of gravity lower than that of our planet (about 1/6). It is precisely for this reason that Alan Shepard, commander of Apollo 14 and the only man to have played golf on the Moon, swears he was able to hit his ball a couple of miles away with a single stroke!

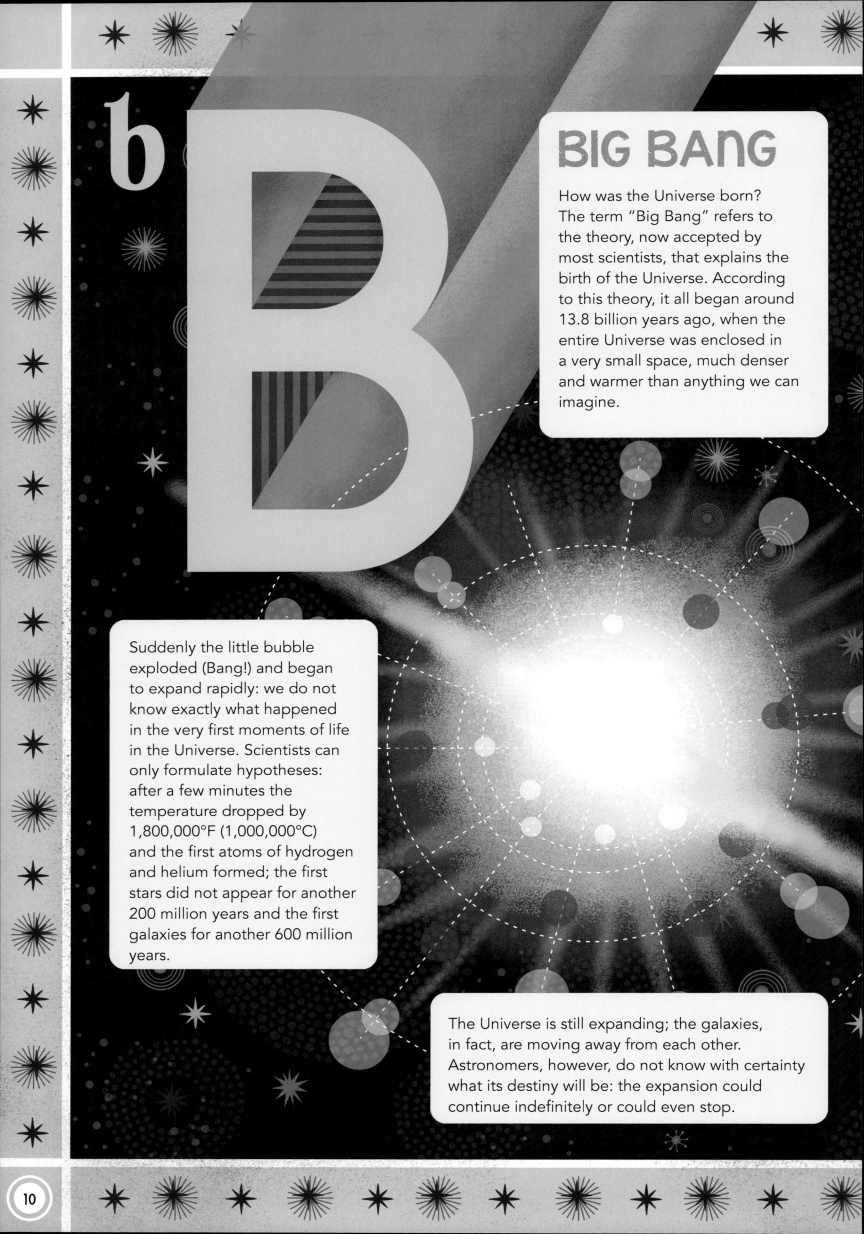

b B BIG BANG

How was the Universe born? The term "Big Bang" refers to the theory, now accepted by most scientists, that explains the birth of the Universe. According to this theory, it all began around 13.8 billion years ago, when the entire Universe was enclosed in a very small space, much denser and warmer than anything we can imagine.

Suddenly the little bubble exploded (Bang!) and began to expand rapidly: we do not know exactly what happened in the very first moments of life in the Universe. Scientists can only formulate hypotheses: after a few minutes the temperature dropped by 1,800,000°F (1,000,000°C) and the first atoms of hydrogen and helium formed; the first stars did not appear for another 200 million years and the first galaxies for another 600 million years.

The Universe is still expanding; the galaxies, in fact, are moving away from each other. Astronomers, however, do not know with certainty what its destiny will be: the expansion could continue indefinitely or could even stop.

BRAHE

Tycho Brahe (1546-1601) was a Danish astronomer famous for his precise observations of the sky without using a telescope. From an early age, he was a fan of astronomy, but his family was against his studies and hired a tutor whose job was to prevent him from observing the sky.

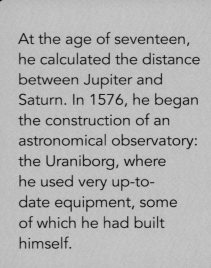

At the age of seventeen, he calculated the distance between Jupiter and Saturn. In 1576, he began the construction of an astronomical observatory: the Uraniborg, where he used very up-to-date equipment, some of which he had built himself.

In 1588, Brahe proposed a new model of the Universe. At that time, most people accepted the theory that the Earth was at the center of the Universe with the Sun, the Moon and the other planets revolved around it. Brahe's idea was that the Earth was motionless at the center, with the Sun and the Moon rotating around it, but that the other planets orbited the Sun. His model of space is called the Tychonic System.

CURIOSITY

Curiosity is the rover (vehicle) that is the protagonist of the NASA mission, Mars Science Laboratory, which is exploring the soil on Mars. Its name was chosen as the result of a competition organized by NASA, attended by students from all over the United States of America. The winner, just 12 years old, was able to visit the laboratory where the Curiosity rover was built and had the honor of signing it before its departure.

The rover left on November 26, 2011 and reached Mars on August 6, 2012. Scientists had to wait 14 minutes to discover the outcome of the landing: this was the amount of time necessary for the radio signal to cover the 154 million miles (248 million kilometers) that separated Earth from Mars on that day.

The rover is about 10 ft long (3 m), weighs 1985 lbs (900 kg) and is equipped with very advanced scientific instruments. The maximum speed that it can reach is about 300 ft/h (90 m/h) and in these five years, it has traveled only 10.5 miles (17 km).

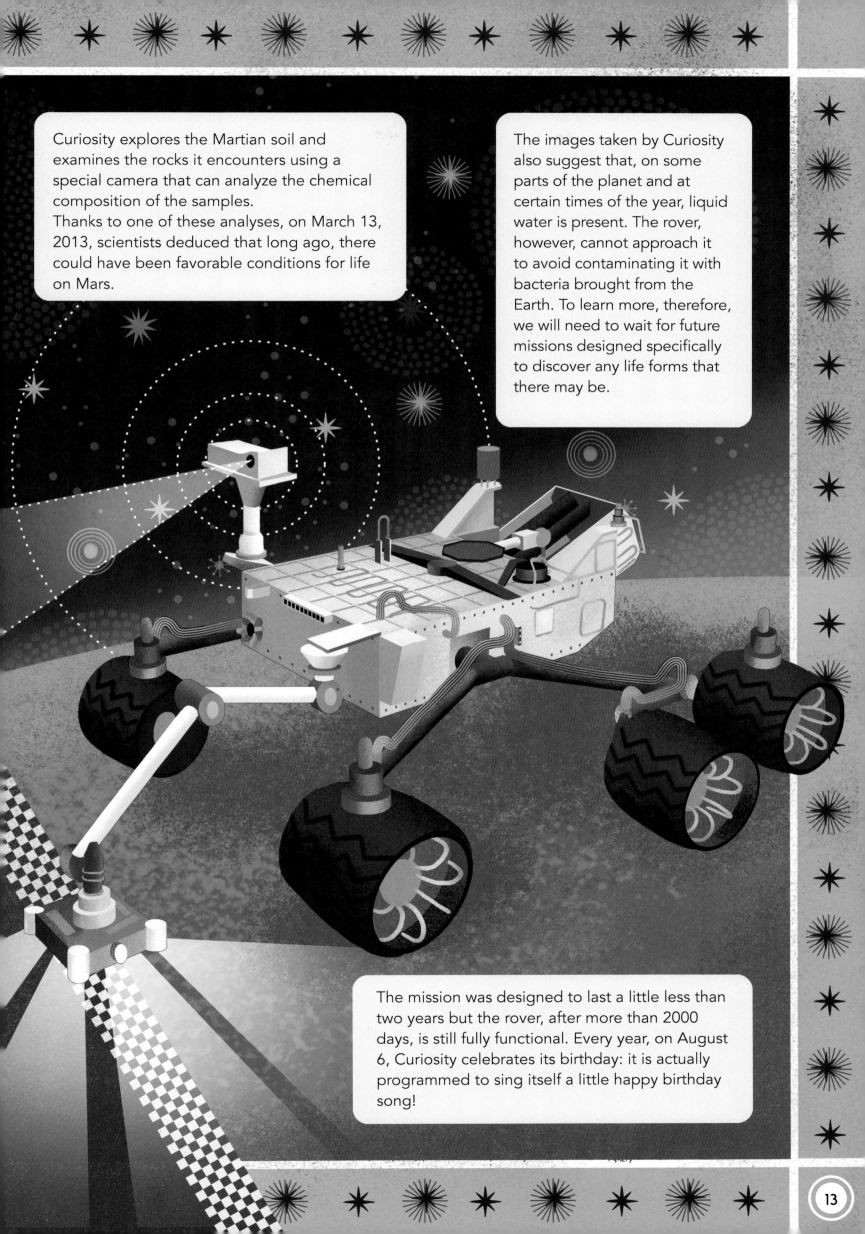

Curiosity explores the Martian soil and examines the rocks it encounters using a special camera that can analyze the chemical composition of the samples.
Thanks to one of these analyses, on March 13, 2013, scientists deduced that long ago, there could have been favorable conditions for life on Mars.

The images taken by Curiosity also suggest that, on some parts of the planet and at certain times of the year, liquid water is present. The rover, however, cannot approach it to avoid contaminating it with bacteria brought from the Earth. To learn more, therefore, we will need to wait for future missions designed specifically to discover any life forms that there may be.

The mission was designed to last a little less than two years but the rover, after more than 2000 days, is still fully functional. Every year, on August 6, Curiosity celebrates its birthday: it is actually programmed to sing itself a little happy birthday song!

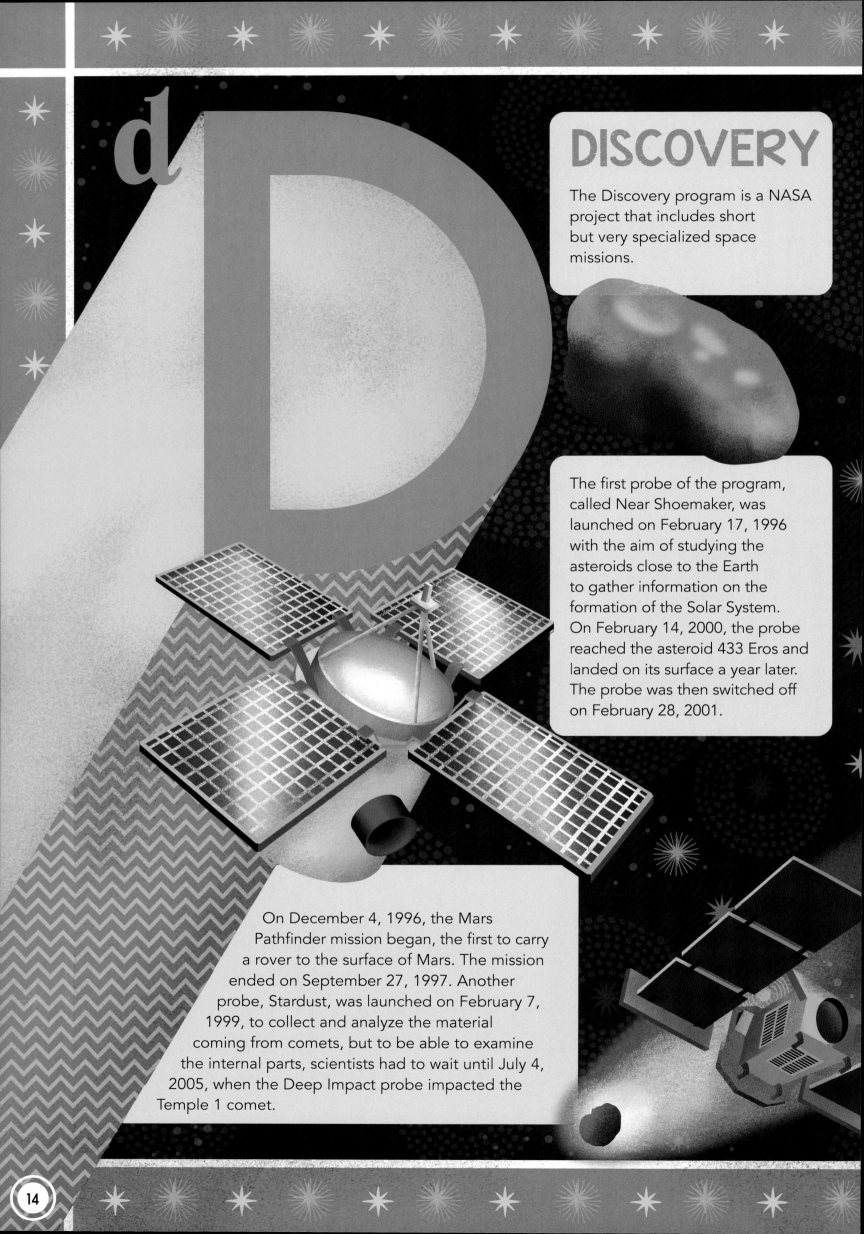

DISCOVERY

The Discovery program is a NASA project that includes short but very specialized space missions.

The first probe of the program, called Near Shoemaker, was launched on February 17, 1996 with the aim of studying the asteroids close to the Earth to gather information on the formation of the Solar System. On February 14, 2000, the probe reached the asteroid 433 Eros and landed on its surface a year later. The probe was then switched off on February 28, 2001.

On December 4, 1996, the Mars Pathfinder mission began, the first to carry a rover to the surface of Mars. The mission ended on September 27, 1997. Another probe, Stardust, was launched on February 7, 1999, to collect and analyze the material coming from comets, but to be able to examine the internal parts, scientists had to wait until July 4, 2005, when the Deep Impact probe impacted the Temple 1 comet.

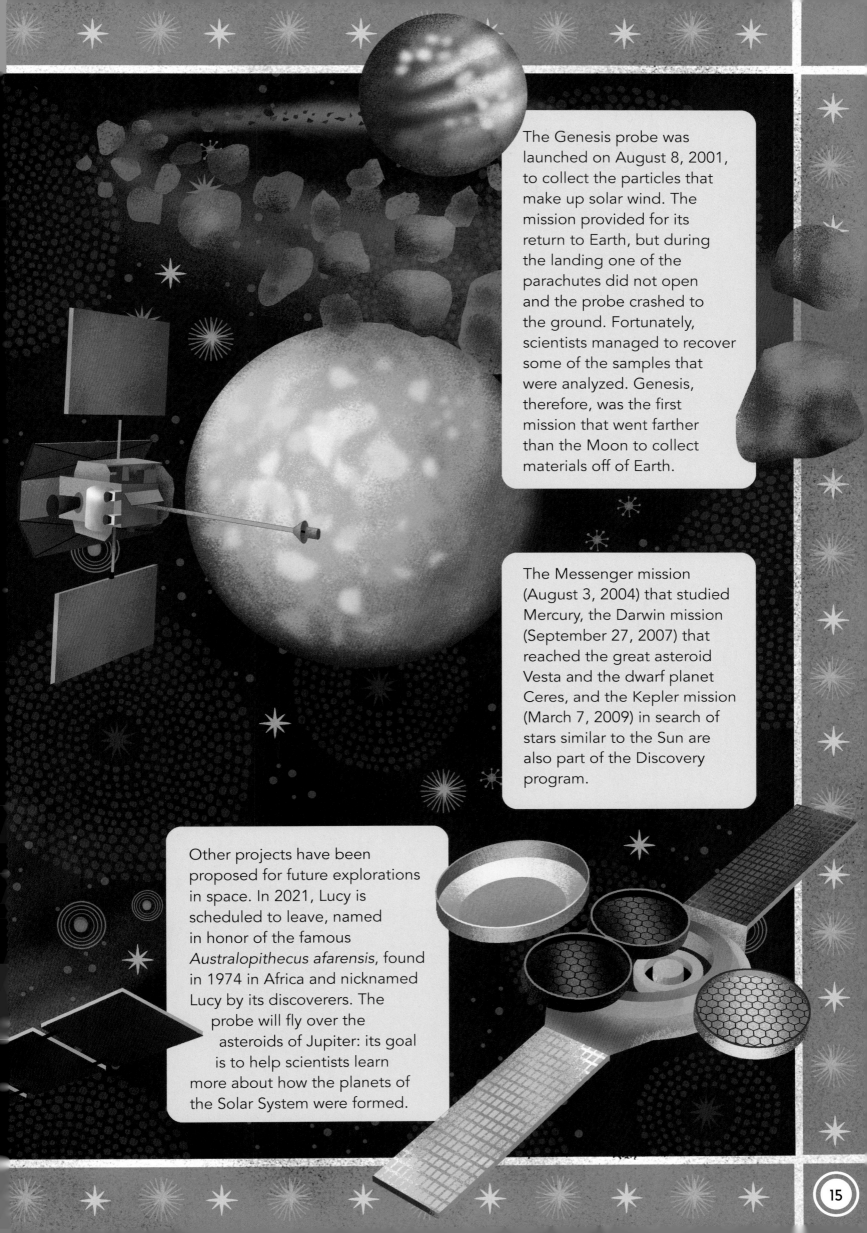

The Genesis probe was launched on August 8, 2001, to collect the particles that make up solar wind. The mission provided for its return to Earth, but during the landing one of the parachutes did not open and the probe crashed to the ground. Fortunately, scientists managed to recover some of the samples that were analyzed. Genesis, therefore, was the first mission that went farther than the Moon to collect materials off of Earth.

The Messenger mission (August 3, 2004) that studied Mercury, the Darwin mission (September 27, 2007) that reached the great asteroid Vesta and the dwarf planet Ceres, and the Kepler mission (March 7, 2009) in search of stars similar to the Sun are also part of the Discovery program.

Other projects have been proposed for future explorations in space. In 2021, Lucy is scheduled to leave, named in honor of the famous *Australopithecus afarensis*, found in 1974 in Africa and nicknamed Lucy by its discoverers. The probe will fly over the asteroids of Jupiter: its goal is to help scientists learn more about how the planets of the Solar System were formed.

ESA

ESA is the abbreviation used to identify the European Space Agency, the organization established in 1975 with the task of uniting and coordinating the space projects of 22 European countries.

The headquarters is in Paris, but ESA has several offices spread across Europe that divide its tasks. The satellite planning center is located in the Netherlands and manned space flights are scheduled there. The astronauts, on the other hand, are trained in Germany, while Italy deals with the missions for the environ mental study of the Earth. The space telescopes are controlled by the Spanish office, where all the data collected by the various projects is also recorded.

In 1983, ESA sent the first astronaut into space and today, together with the Russian Space Agency and NASA, trains and launches astronauts to the International Space Station. The first European rocket, the Ariane 1, was launched on December 24, 1979. Today, the most powerful ESA rocket is the Arian 5, capable of carrying 21,000 kilograms of heavy satellites into space. Human flights, on the other hand, are achieved thanks to the Russian rocket Soyuz.

Thanks to the expertise of many nations, ESA has distinguished itself in the exploration of the Solar System: the discovery of frozen water beneath the surface of Mars was thanks to ESA and it has put the SOHO satellite into space with the task of sending the images of the surface of the Sun. The object that has landed at the farthest point from the Earth is also European: on January 14, 2005, the Huygens probe descended onto Titan, one of the moons of Saturn, after a journey of more than seven years.

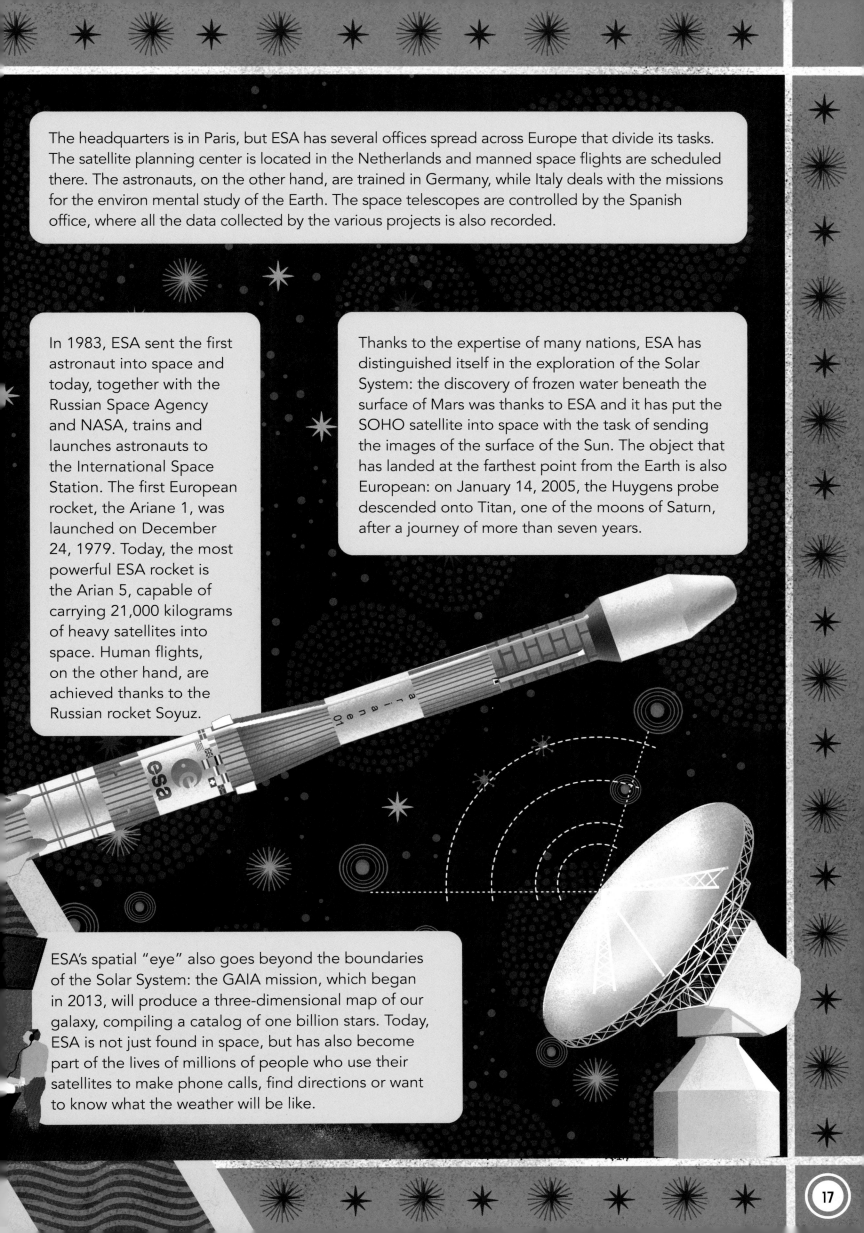

ESA's spatial "eye" also goes beyond the boundaries of the Solar System: the GAIA mission, which began in 2013, will produce a three-dimensional map of our galaxy, compiling a catalog of one billion stars. Today, ESA is not just found in space, but has also become part of the lives of millions of people who use their satellites to make phone calls, find directions or want to know what the weather will be like.

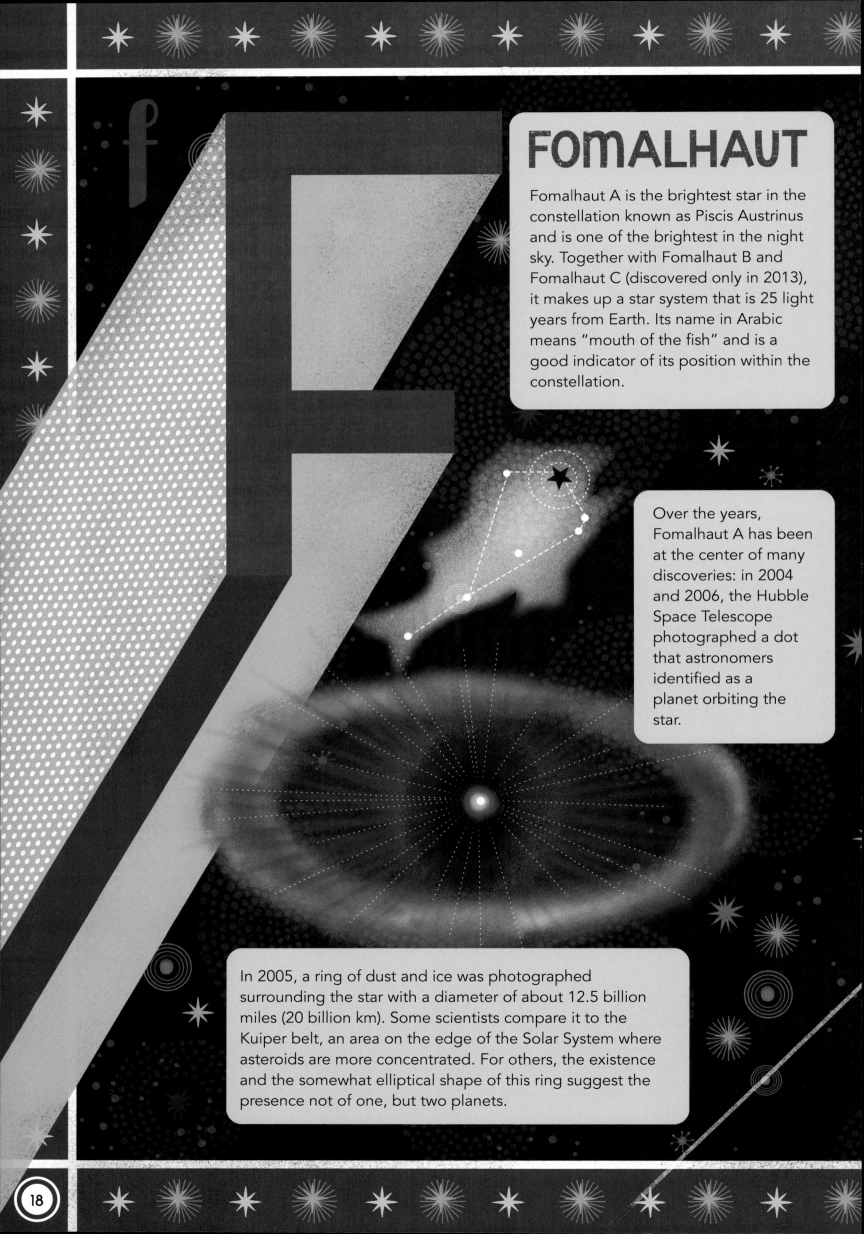

FOMALHAUT

Fomalhaut A is the brightest star in the constellation known as Piscis Austrinus and is one of the brightest in the night sky. Together with Fomalhaut B and Fomalhaut C (discovered only in 2013), it makes up a star system that is 25 light years from Earth. Its name in Arabic means "mouth of the fish" and is a good indicator of its position within the constellation.

Over the years, Fomalhaut A has been at the center of many discoveries: in 2004 and 2006, the Hubble Space Telescope photographed a dot that astronomers identified as a planet orbiting the star.

In 2005, a ring of dust and ice was photographed surrounding the star with a diameter of about 12.5 billion miles (20 billion km). Some scientists compare it to the Kuiper belt, an area on the edge of the Solar System where asteroids are more concentrated. For others, the existence and the somewhat elliptical shape of this ring suggest the presence not of one, but two planets.

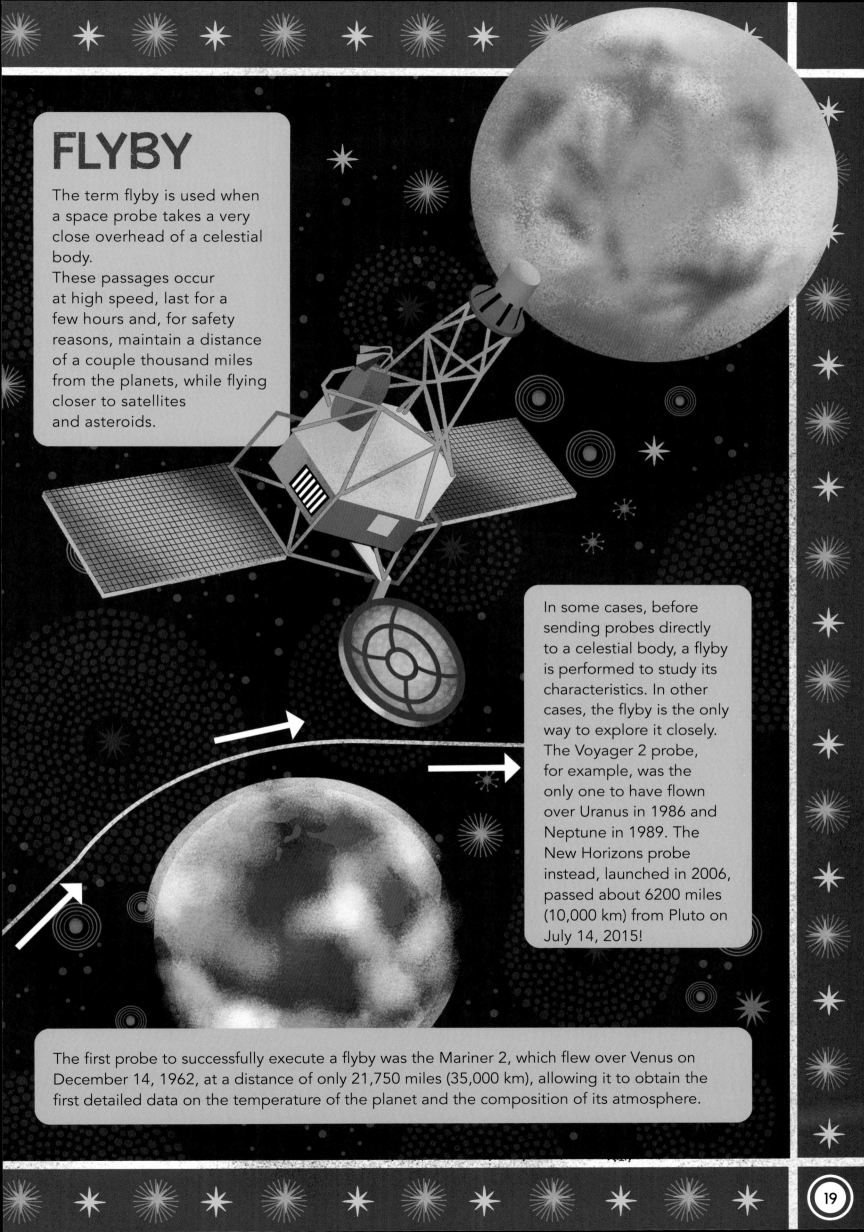

FLYBY

The term flyby is used when a space probe takes a very close overhead of a celestial body.
These passages occur at high speed, last for a few hours and, for safety reasons, maintain a distance of a couple thousand miles from the planets, while flying closer to satellites and asteroids.

In some cases, before sending probes directly to a celestial body, a flyby is performed to study its characteristics. In other cases, the flyby is the only way to explore it closely. The Voyager 2 probe, for example, was the only one to have flown over Uranus in 1986 and Neptune in 1989. The New Horizons probe instead, launched in 2006, passed about 6200 miles (10,000 km) from Pluto on July 14, 2015!

The first probe to successfully execute a flyby was the Mariner 2, which flew over Venus on December 14, 1962, at a distance of only 21,750 miles (35,000 km), allowing it to obtain the first detailed data on the temperature of the planet and the composition of its atmosphere.

GAGARIN

Launching on April 12, 1961 at 9:07 am, Jurij Gagarin was the first human being sent into orbit around the Earth! Jurij, a Russian aviation pilot, was chosen out of 3461 aspiring cosmonauts and had the honor of seeing our planet from space before anyone else.

After the capsule lid was closed, he simply said, "Let's, go" and, once in orbit, he exclaimed the famous phrase: "The Earth is blue... how wonderful... it's beautiful!" During his flight aboard the Vostok 1, he reached a height of 187.8 miles (302 km) and a speed of 17,000 mph (27,400 km/h)!

108 minutes after the launch, 88 of which were used to pass into orbit, he was ejected from his capsule and landed with a parachute on a farm, where he was "welcomed" by a frightened peasant named Anna Taktatova, along with her daughter and a calf. This was the first and only space flight for Jurij Gagarin, but he left a bit of himself in space: his name was given to a lunar crater and an asteroid.

g G

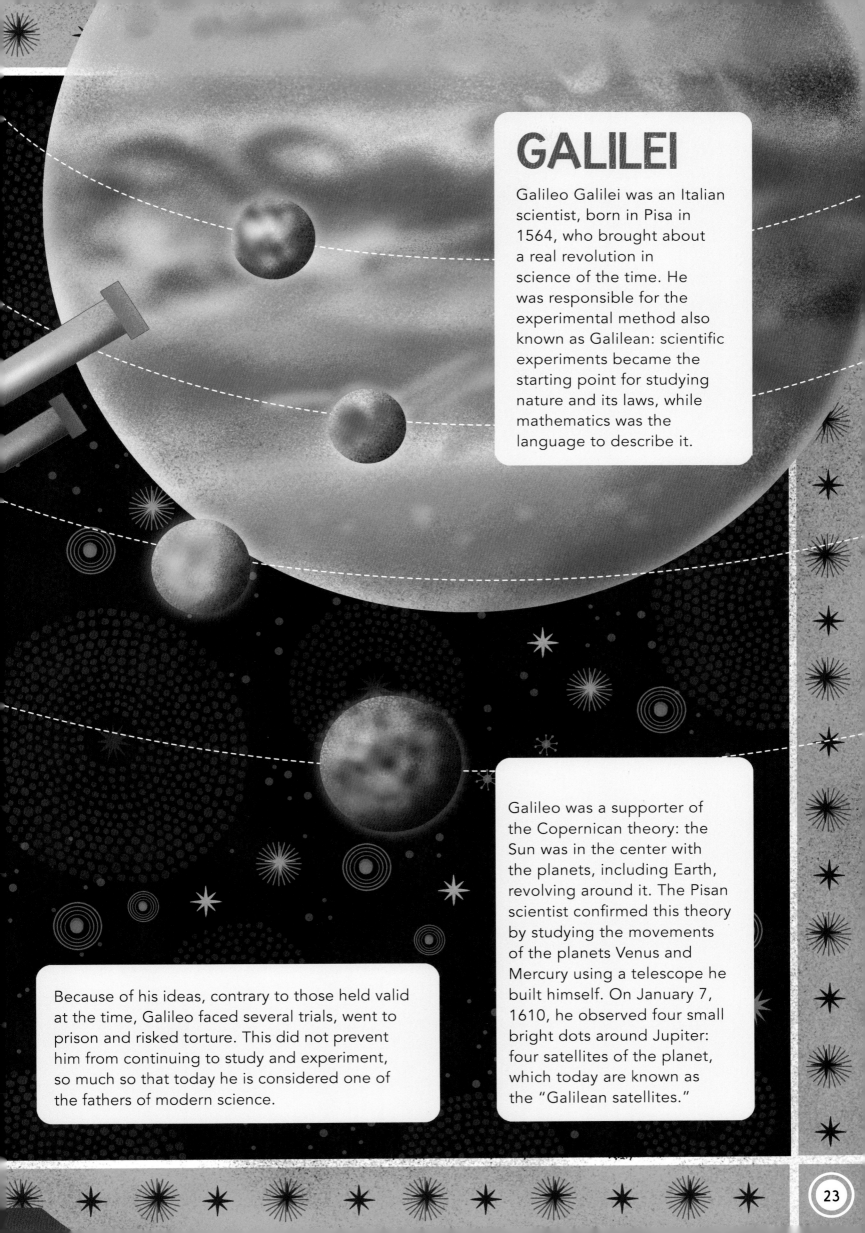

GALILEI

Galileo Galilei was an Italian scientist, born in Pisa in 1564, who brought about a real revolution in science of the time. He was responsible for the experimental method also known as Galilean: scientific experiments became the starting point for studying nature and its laws, while mathematics was the language to describe it.

Galileo was a supporter of the Copernican theory: the Sun was in the center with the planets, including Earth, revolving around it. The Pisan scientist confirmed this theory by studying the movements of the planets Venus and Mercury using a telescope he built himself. On January 7, 1610, he observed four small bright dots around Jupiter: four satellites of the planet, which today are known as the "Galilean satellites."

Because of his ideas, contrary to those held valid at the time, Galileo faced several trials, went to prison and risked torture. This did not prevent him from continuing to study and experiment, so much so that today he is considered one of the fathers of modern science.

h HALLEY

HALLEY

Halley is the name given to one of the most brilliant comets ever known, in honor of Edmond Halley, the first astronomer who studied it in the sixteenth century and predicted its return by the end of 1758. It is a periodic comet: along its very elongated orbit, it becomes visible to Earth every 76 years.

The first official sighting of Halley's Comet was recorded by Chinese astronomers in 240 BC. Its passage in 1456 brought it very close to Earth and the comet appeared in the sky like a gigantic scimitar, frightening terribly those who watched it. The biggest spectacle, however, occurred in 837, when its tail crossed the night sky from horizon to horizon.

The first photographs of the comet date back to its passage in 1910, but it was only in 1986 that it was closely observed: several European, Russian, Chinese and American probes were launched into space with the aim of studying it. The next time it returns to visit Earth will be in 2062.

h HUBBLE

The Hubble Space Telescope (HST) is one of the largest and most famous space telescopes. It was launched in 1990 and orbits about 336 miles (540 km) from Earth's surface, allowing it to scan the universe without disturbances due to the atmosphere.

Its highly technological instrumentation today allows it to take photographs and make analyses using ultraviolet and infrared light but, when it was originally put into orbit, scientists realized that its "eye", a mirror 7.9 ft (2.4 m) in diameter, had a small flaw. In 1993, a space mission was launched to correct the problem with a series of additional mirrors. Thanks to its new "glasses", the telescope has sent more than 700,000 images to the ground and will continue to explore the universe until at least 2030.

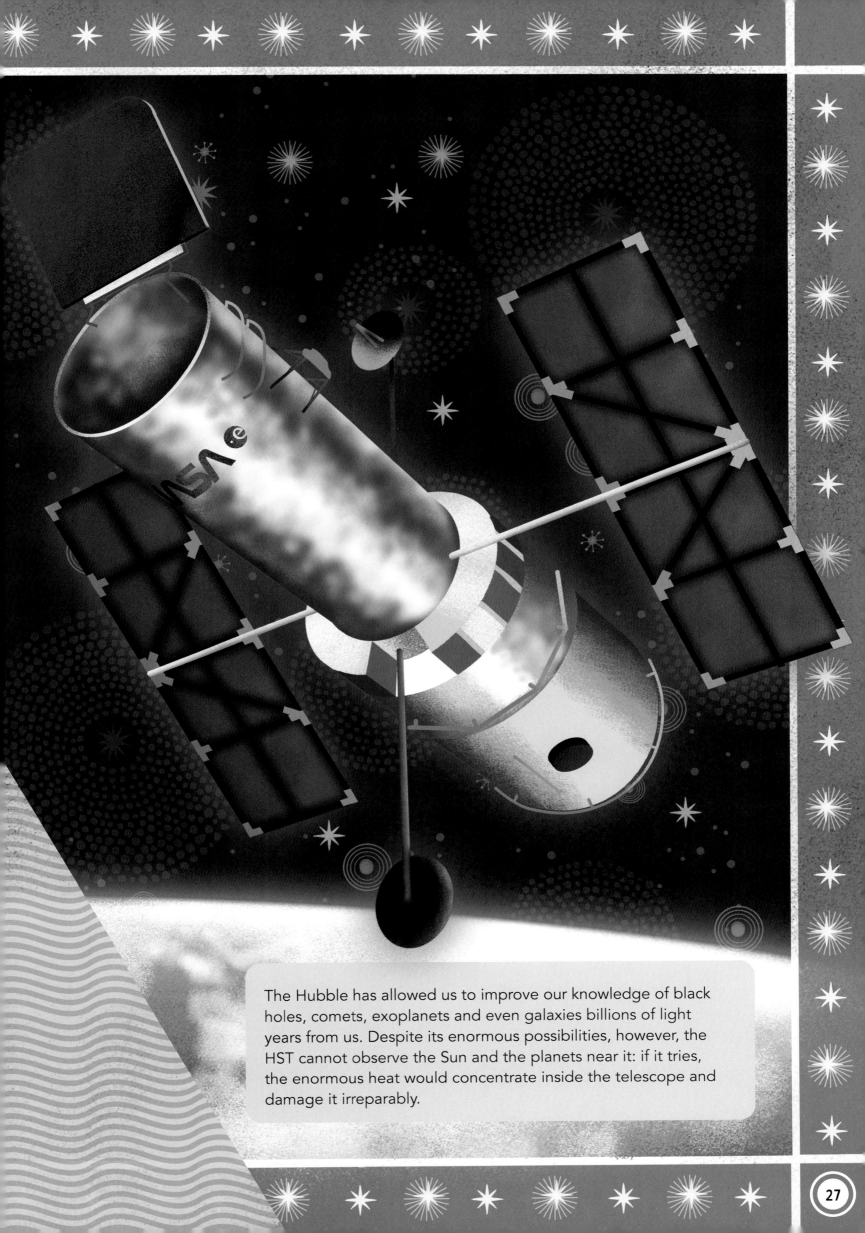

The Hubble has allowed us to improve our knowledge of black holes, comets, exoplanets and even galaxies billions of light years from us. Despite its enormous possibilities, however, the HST cannot observe the Sun and the planets near it: if it tries, the enormous heat would concentrate inside the telescope and damage it irreparably.

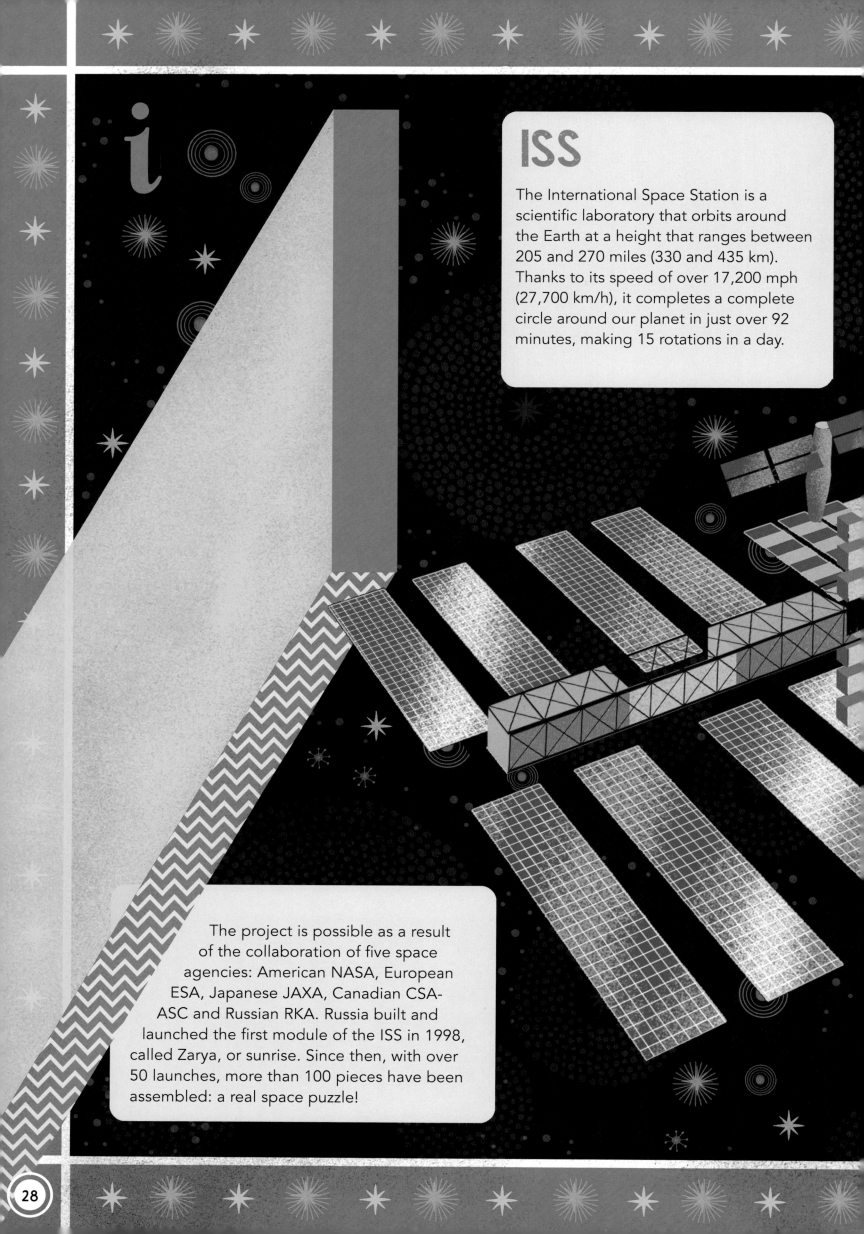

ISS

The International Space Station is a scientific laboratory that orbits around the Earth at a height that ranges between 205 and 270 miles (330 and 435 km). Thanks to its speed of over 17,200 mph (27,700 km/h), it completes a complete circle around our planet in just over 92 minutes, making 15 rotations in a day.

The project is possible as a result of the collaboration of five space agencies: American NASA, European ESA, Japanese JAXA, Canadian CSA-ASC and Russian RKA. Russia built and launched the first module of the ISS in 1998, called Zarya, or sunrise. Since then, with over 50 launches, more than 100 pieces have been assembled: a real space puzzle!

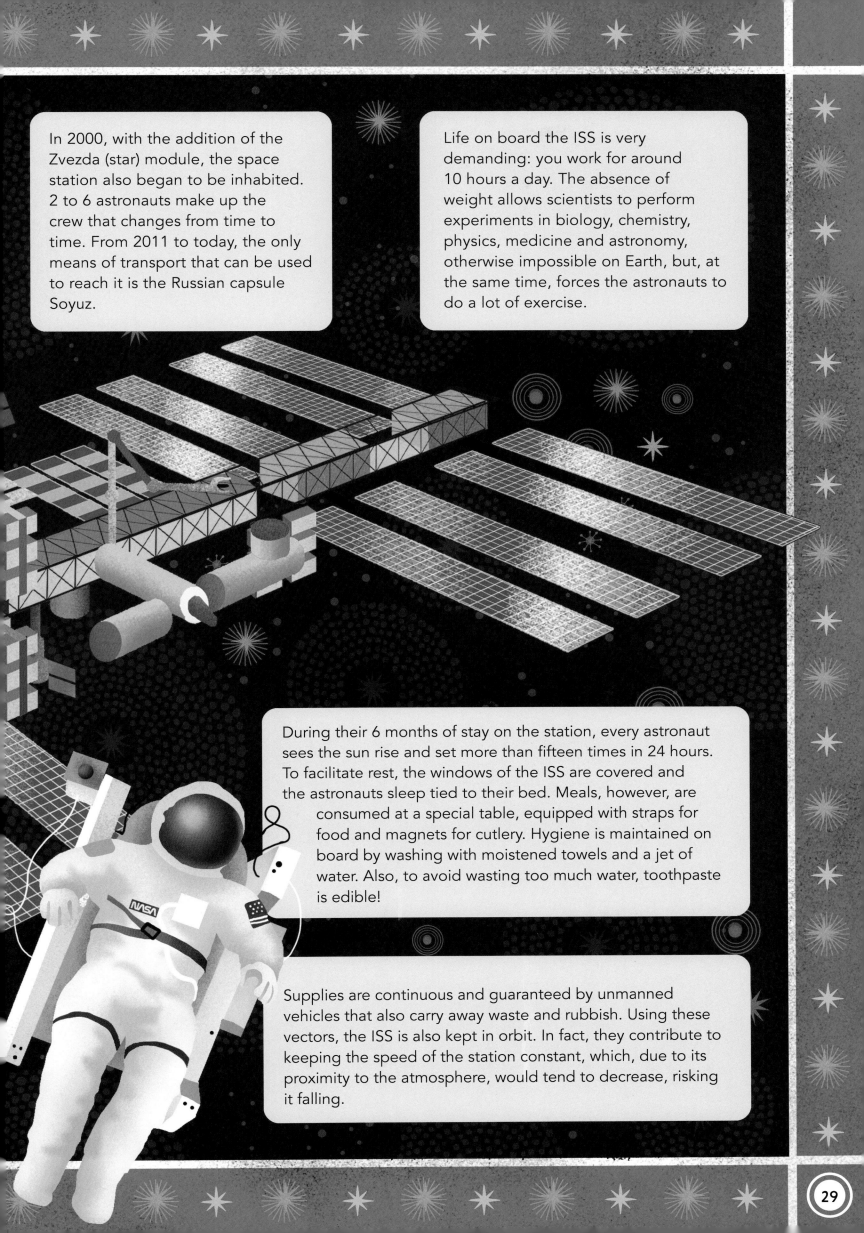

In 2000, with the addition of the Zvezda (star) module, the space station also began to be inhabited. 2 to 6 astronauts make up the crew that changes from time to time. From 2011 to today, the only means of transport that can be used to reach it is the Russian capsule Soyuz.

Life on board the ISS is very demanding: you work for around 10 hours a day. The absence of weight allows scientists to perform experiments in biology, chemistry, physics, medicine and astronomy, otherwise impossible on Earth, but, at the same time, forces the astronauts to do a lot of exercise.

During their 6 months of stay on the station, every astronaut sees the sun rise and set more than fifteen times in 24 hours. To facilitate rest, the windows of the ISS are covered and the astronauts sleep tied to their bed. Meals, however, are consumed at a special table, equipped with straps for food and magnets for cutlery. Hygiene is maintained on board by washing with moistened towels and a jet of water. Also, to avoid wasting too much water, toothpaste is edible!

Supplies are continuous and guaranteed by unmanned vehicles that also carry away waste and rubbish. Using these vectors, the ISS is also kept in orbit. In fact, they contribute to keeping the speed of the station constant, which, due to its proximity to the atmosphere, would tend to decrease, risking it falling.

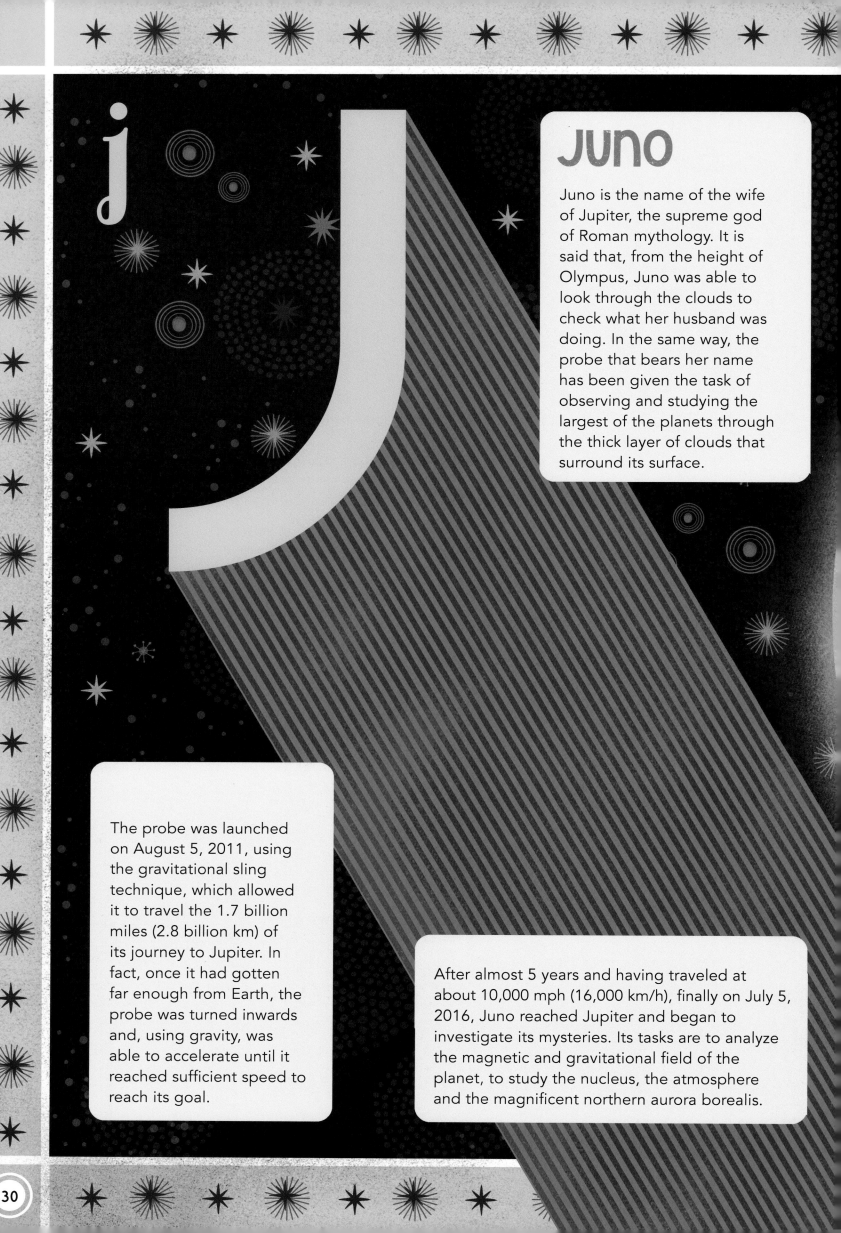

JUNO

Juno is the name of the wife of Jupiter, the supreme god of Roman mythology. It is said that, from the height of Olympus, Juno was able to look through the clouds to check what her husband was doing. In the same way, the probe that bears her name has been given the task of observing and studying the largest of the planets through the thick layer of clouds that surround its surface.

The probe was launched on August 5, 2011, using the gravitational sling technique, which allowed it to travel the 1.7 billion miles (2.8 billion km) of its journey to Jupiter. In fact, once it had gotten far enough from Earth, the probe was turned inwards and, using gravity, was able to accelerate until it reached sufficient speed to reach its goal.

After almost 5 years and having traveled at about 10,000 mph (16,000 km/h), finally on July 5, 2016, Juno reached Jupiter and began to investigate its mysteries. Its tasks are to analyze the magnetic and gravitational field of the planet, to study the nucleus, the atmosphere and the magnificent northern aurora borealis.

The mission program stated that, before its conclusion in 2018, the probe would have orbited around Jupiter 57 times. Due to an engine failure, however, the safety mode has been activated and as a result, it will complete fewer orbits than planned. The mission, however, will probably not be affected because, by consuming less energy, the probe will last longer.

Jupiter is a gas giant composed of hydrogen and helium, so large that it could hold about 1300 planets as large as the Earth. Precisely because of its size, Juno takes 53 days to complete a full orbit. On July 10, 2017, the spacecraft moved 2175 miles (3500 km) away from the surface, capturing spectacular images of the Great Red Spot, a storm three times larger than Earth, which has disrupted the planet's surface for over 300 years.

In addition to scientific instrumentation, Juno also carried three Lego® characters that depict Galileo Galilei, Jupiter and Juno.

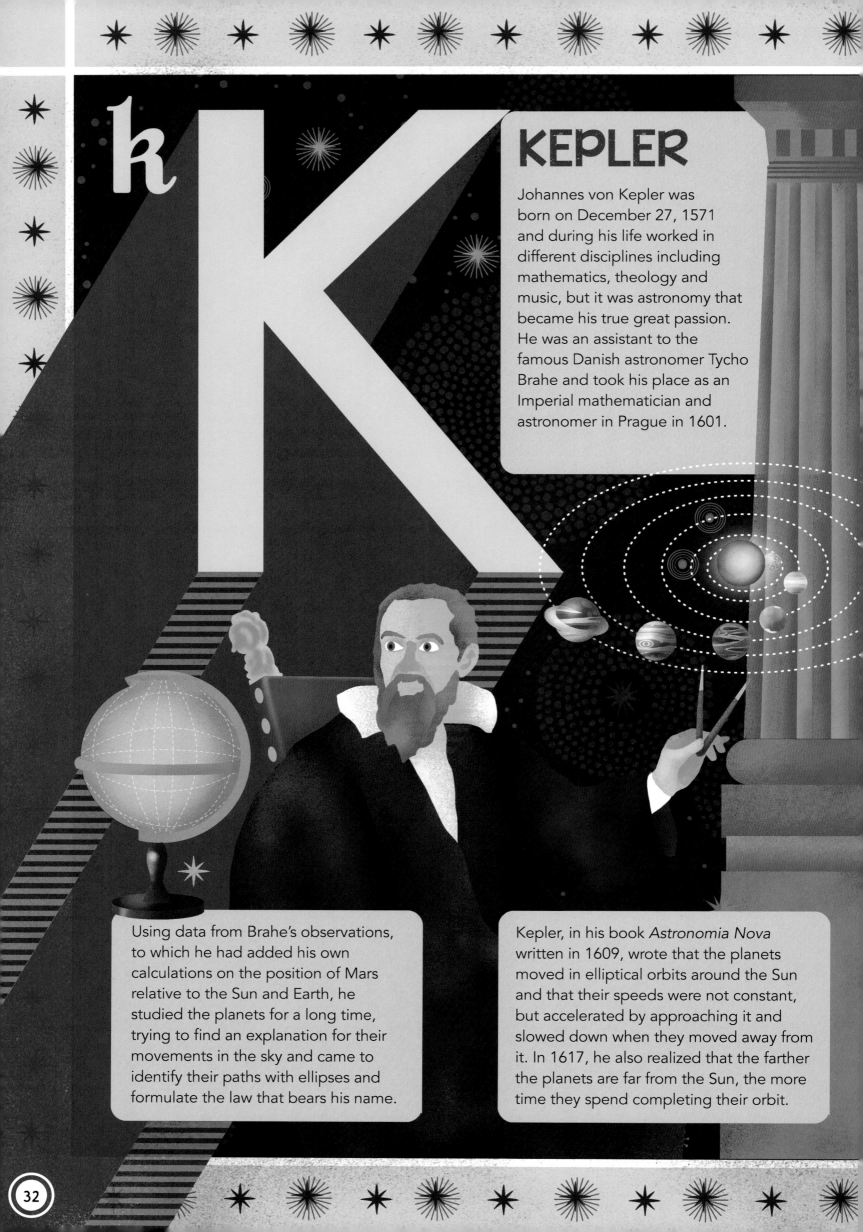

KEPLER

Johannes von Kepler was born on December 27, 1571 and during his life worked in different disciplines including mathematics, theology and music, but it was astronomy that became his true great passion. He was an assistant to the famous Danish astronomer Tycho Brahe and took his place as an Imperial mathematician and astronomer in Prague in 1601.

Using data from Brahe's observations, to which he had added his own calculations on the position of Mars relative to the Sun and Earth, he studied the planets for a long time, trying to find an explanation for their movements in the sky and came to identify their paths with ellipses and formulate the law that bears his name.

Kepler, in his book *Astronomia Nova* written in 1609, wrote that the planets moved in elliptical orbits around the Sun and that their speeds were not constant, but accelerated by approaching it and slowed down when they moved away from it. In 1617, he also realized that the farther the planets are far from the Sun, the more time they spend completing their orbit.

KUIPER

The Kuiper belt is an area that lies on the edge of the Solar System, beyond the planet Neptune, 2.8 billion miles (4.5 billion km) from the Sun. It takes its name from the astronomer Gerard Kuiper, who in 1951 hypothesized that some comets had their origin in this region.

The objects present here are not easily visible: in fact, if we exclude Pluto, the first one was only identified in 1992 using powerful telescopes. Since then hundreds of other small frozen celestial bodies have been discovered which are probably the remains of materials that failed to aggregate to form the planets when the Solar System was born.

The largest objects in the Kuiper belt are the dwarf planets Pluto and Eris, but this area still hides many mysteries! For this reason, in 2006, the New Horizons probe was launched, which, after its flyby of Pluto in 2015, continued its journey and will reach a small frozen body about 1 billion miles (1.5 billion km) away from it in 2019!

LAIKA

The first explorers in space were animals. On November 3, 1957, aboard the Russian Sputnik 2 satellite, a little dog Laika, was sent into space: it was therefore the first living being to be launched into orbit around Earth! There were actually three little dogs trained for the mission, but in the end, Laika was the one chosen for space flight. Its real name was Kudriavka, but it is known worldwide as Laika.

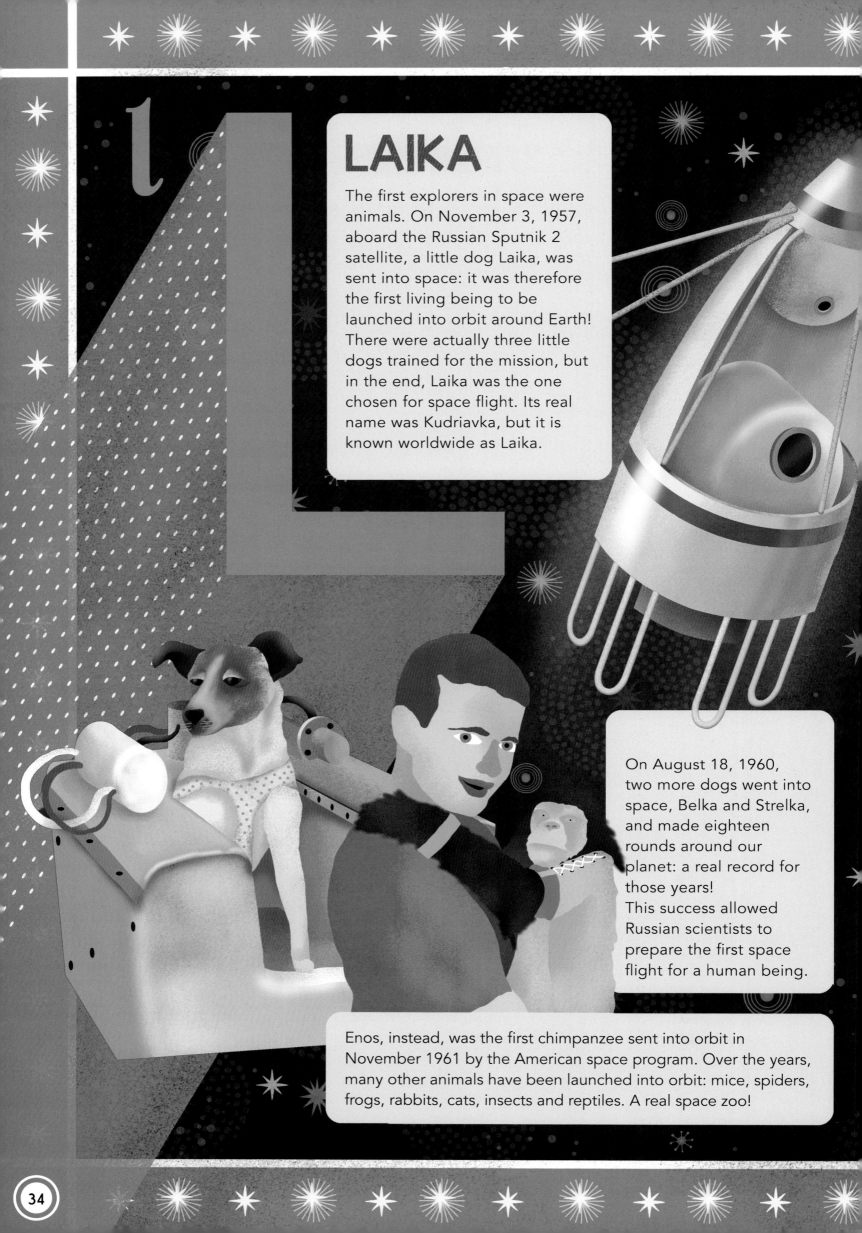

On August 18, 1960, two more dogs went into space, Belka and Strelka, and made eighteen rounds around our planet: a real record for those years!
This success allowed Russian scientists to prepare the first space flight for a human being.

Enos, instead, was the first chimpanzee sent into orbit in November 1961 by the American space program. Over the years, many other animals have been launched into orbit: mice, spiders, frogs, rabbits, cats, insects and reptiles. A real space zoo!

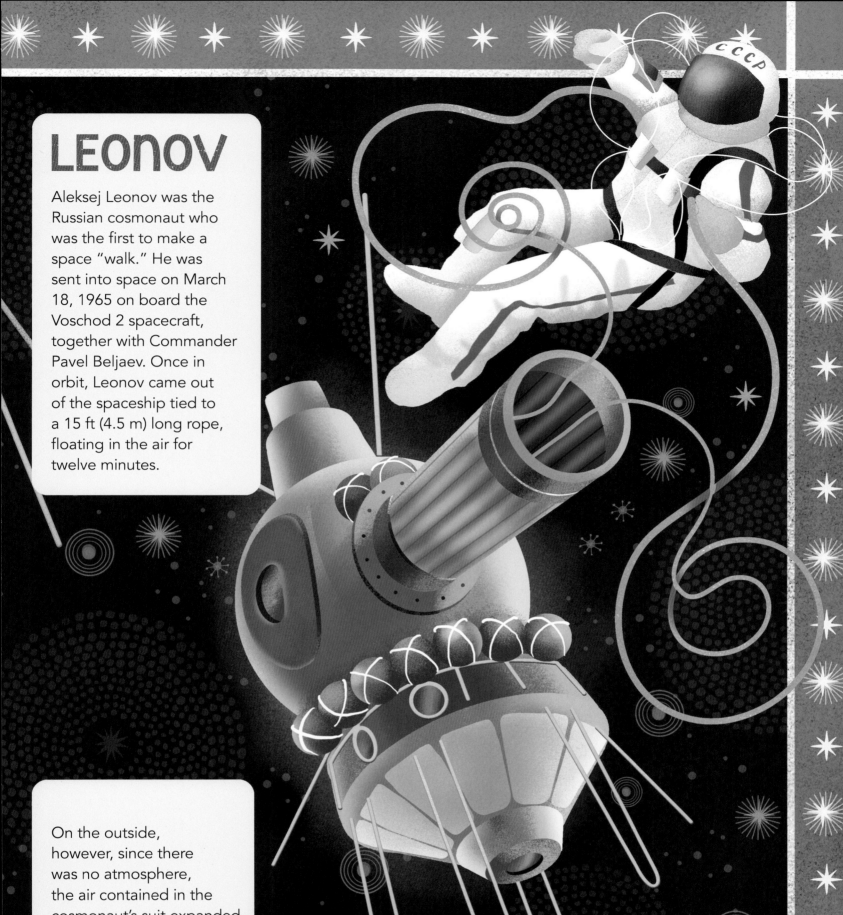

LEONOV

Aleksej Leonov was the Russian cosmonaut who was the first to make a space "walk." He was sent into space on March 18, 1965 on board the Voschod 2 spacecraft, together with Commander Pavel Beljaev. Once in orbit, Leonov came out of the spaceship tied to a 15 ft (4.5 m) long rope, floating in the air for twelve minutes.

On the outside, however, since there was no atmosphere, the air contained in the cosmonaut's suit expanded more than expected, inflating it so much that it no longer passed through the door of the spacecraft. Leonov solved the problem by deflating his suit like a balloon! He risked his life, but in the end everything went well.

Even the return to Earth was a bit unlucky for the two cosmonauts: due to a breakdown, the Voschod 2 spacecraft landed 930 miles (1500 km) away from the intended landing point, in a remote snowy forest. Leonov and Beljaev were not rescued until two days after landing and were forced to remain at a temperature of -22°F (-30°C).

MARS EXPRESS

Mars Express is an ESA mission, launched on June 2, 2003, with the task of studying Mars. The name derives from the fact that, given the particular position of Mars compared to Earth, the travel time would have been the shortest possible up to that moment: the two planets, in fact, had never been so close in the last 60,000 years!

Mars, because of its characteristics, is the only planet on which one can think of finding forms of life, currently or in the past. It is a rocky planet, has a diameter that is about half that of the Earth and, given its distance from the Sun, the average surface temperature of -81°F (-63°C) is not very different from those recorded in the polar areas of the Earth.

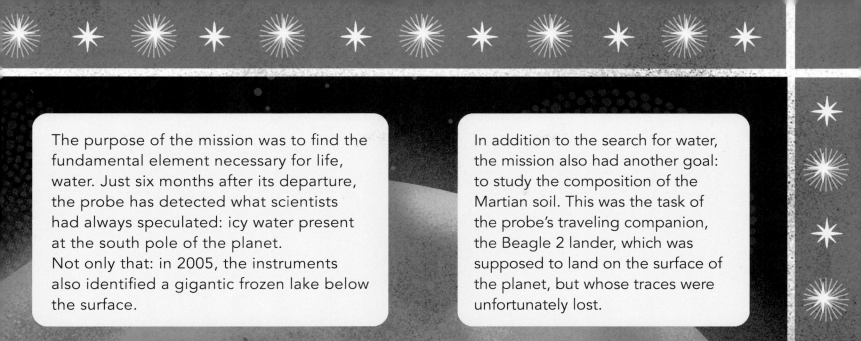

The purpose of the mission was to find the fundamental element necessary for life, water. Just six months after its departure, the probe has detected what scientists had always speculated: icy water present at the south pole of the planet.
Not only that: in 2005, the instruments also identified a gigantic frozen lake below the surface.

In addition to the search for water, the mission also had another goal: to study the composition of the Martian soil. This was the task of the probe's traveling companion, the Beagle 2 lander, which was supposed to land on the surface of the planet, but whose traces were unfortunately lost.

It was only 11 years after the departure of the mission, thanks to the images of the Mars Reconnaissance Orbiter (a NASA probe), that ESA rediscovered its lost lander. Unfortunately, its solar panels did not opened properly and, as it is not getting enough energy, Beagle 2 will never work.

The instruments on board the Mars Express are incredibly sensitive and allow us to identify the presence of even a few molecules of compounds present in the Martian atmosphere. Using them, it has been possible to detect methane and this is considered by some scientists as proof of the existence of primitive micro-organisms on the planet.

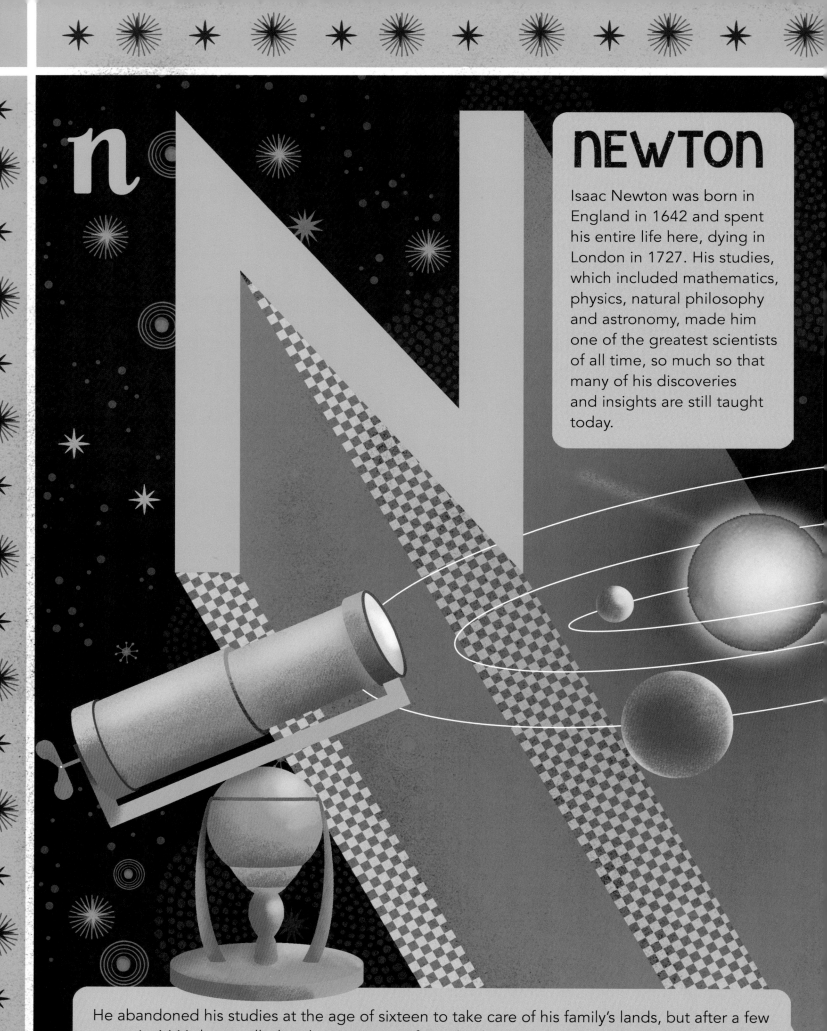

NEWTON

Isaac Newton was born in England in 1642 and spent his entire life here, dying in London in 1727. His studies, which included mathematics, physics, natural philosophy and astronomy, made him one of the greatest scientists of all time, so much so that many of his discoveries and insights are still taught today.

He abandoned his studies at the age of sixteen to take care of his family's lands, but after a few years, in 1661, he enrolled at the University of Cambridge, where, however, he did not become interested in the normal course of studies. Everything changed with the arrival of the plague and the consequent closure of the College. Forced to continue his studies alone, Newton developed his first mathematical theories.

In 1969, he was appointed professor of mathematics and in the following years, he devoted himself to the study of light: it is his merit if today we know that white light is made up of all the colors and that these can be separated from one another by passing a ray of light through a prism.

The results of Newton's studies, the basis of many astronomical theories, are included in his greatest work, consisting of three volumes. In this work, the scientist explains the laws that govern the motion of the planets around the Sun and of the satellites around their planets.

His most famous law, contained in the third volume, is known as the "law of universal gravitation." With it, Newton proved that the orbits of the planets are elliptical in shape, he was able to correctly explain the movements of comets and also to mathematically demonstrate the laws of Kepler.

Tradition has it that his insights on gravity and the motion of the planets are due to a small accident: an apple falling from the tree under which Newton was resting, hit him on the head. This episode never actually occurred, but this legend shows how the scientist carefully observed nature before describing it.

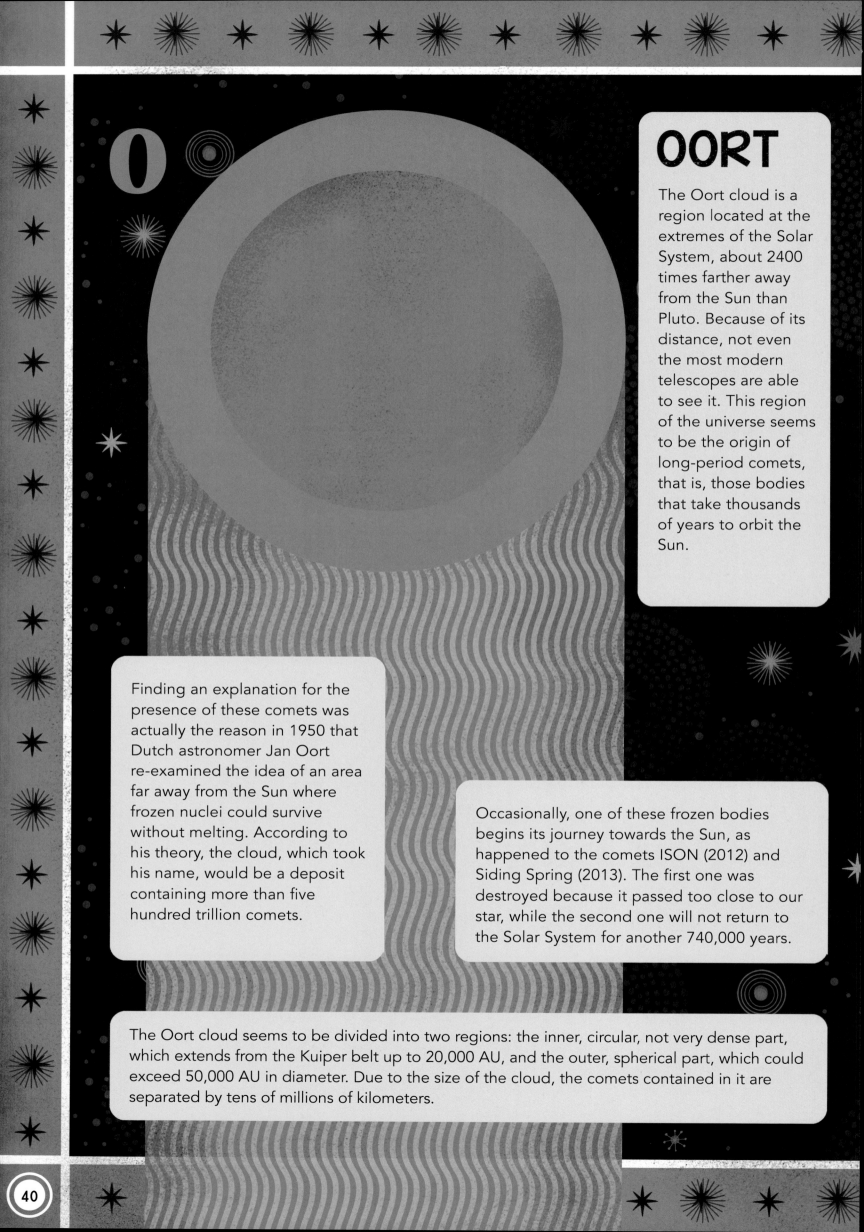

OORT

The Oort cloud is a region located at the extremes of the Solar System, about 2400 times farther away from the Sun than Pluto. Because of its distance, not even the most modern telescopes are able to see it. This region of the universe seems to be the origin of long-period comets, that is, those bodies that take thousands of years to orbit the Sun.

Finding an explanation for the presence of these comets was actually the reason in 1950 that Dutch astronomer Jan Oort re-examined the idea of an area far away from the Sun where frozen nuclei could survive without melting. According to his theory, the cloud, which took his name, would be a deposit containing more than five hundred trillion comets.

Occasionally, one of these frozen bodies begins its journey towards the Sun, as happened to the comets ISON (2012) and Siding Spring (2013). The first one was destroyed because it passed too close to our star, while the second one will not return to the Solar System for another 740,000 years.

The Oort cloud seems to be divided into two regions: the inner, circular, not very dense part, which extends from the Kuiper belt up to 20,000 AU, and the outer, spherical part, which could exceed 50,000 AU in diameter. Due to the size of the cloud, the comets contained in it are separated by tens of millions of kilometers.

Although it is not possible to see the Cloud directly, objects, besides the comets, that could belong to it, like the planetoid Sedna, have been seen, even though not all astronomers agree on its origin. The presence inside the cloud of a giant, gaseous planet, Thyche, was hypothesized, but later denied.

The Voyager 1 probe, which is about 13 billion miles (21 billion km) from Earth, will take another 300 years to reach the Oort cloud and more than 30,000 years to cross it completely! Unfortunately, however, it will no longer be able to communicate with our planet!

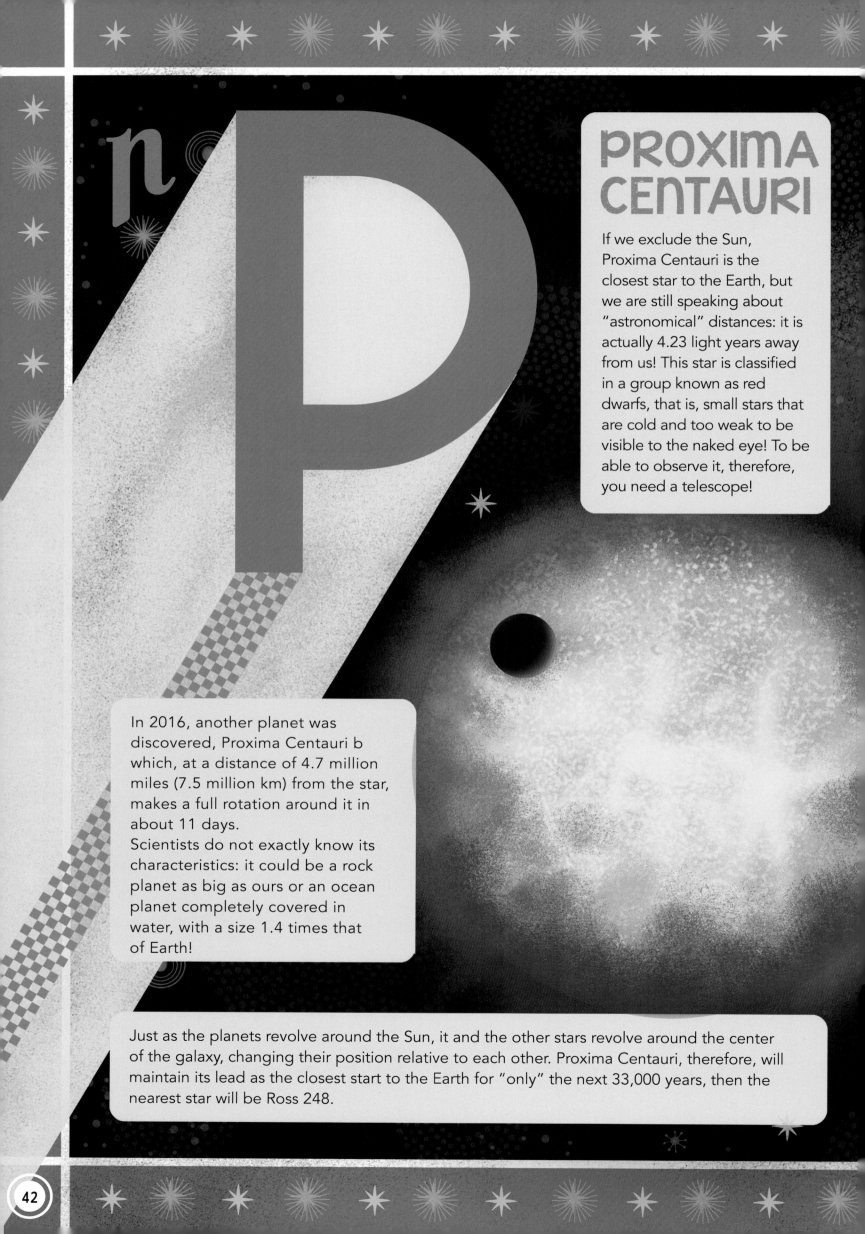

PROXIMA CENTAURI

If we exclude the Sun, Proxima Centauri is the closest star to the Earth, but we are still speaking about "astronomical" distances: it is actually 4.23 light years away from us! This star is classified in a group known as red dwarfs, that is, small stars that are cold and too weak to be visible to the naked eye! To be able to observe it, therefore, you need a telescope!

In 2016, another planet was discovered, Proxima Centauri b which, at a distance of 4.7 million miles (7.5 million km) from the star, makes a full rotation around it in about 11 days.
Scientists do not exactly know its characteristics: it could be a rock planet as big as ours or an ocean planet completely covered in water, with a size 1.4 times that of Earth!

Just as the planets revolve around the Sun, it and the other stars revolve around the center of the galaxy, changing their position relative to each other. Proxima Centauri, therefore, will maintain its lead as the closest start to the Earth for "only" the next 33,000 years, then the nearest star will be Ross 248.

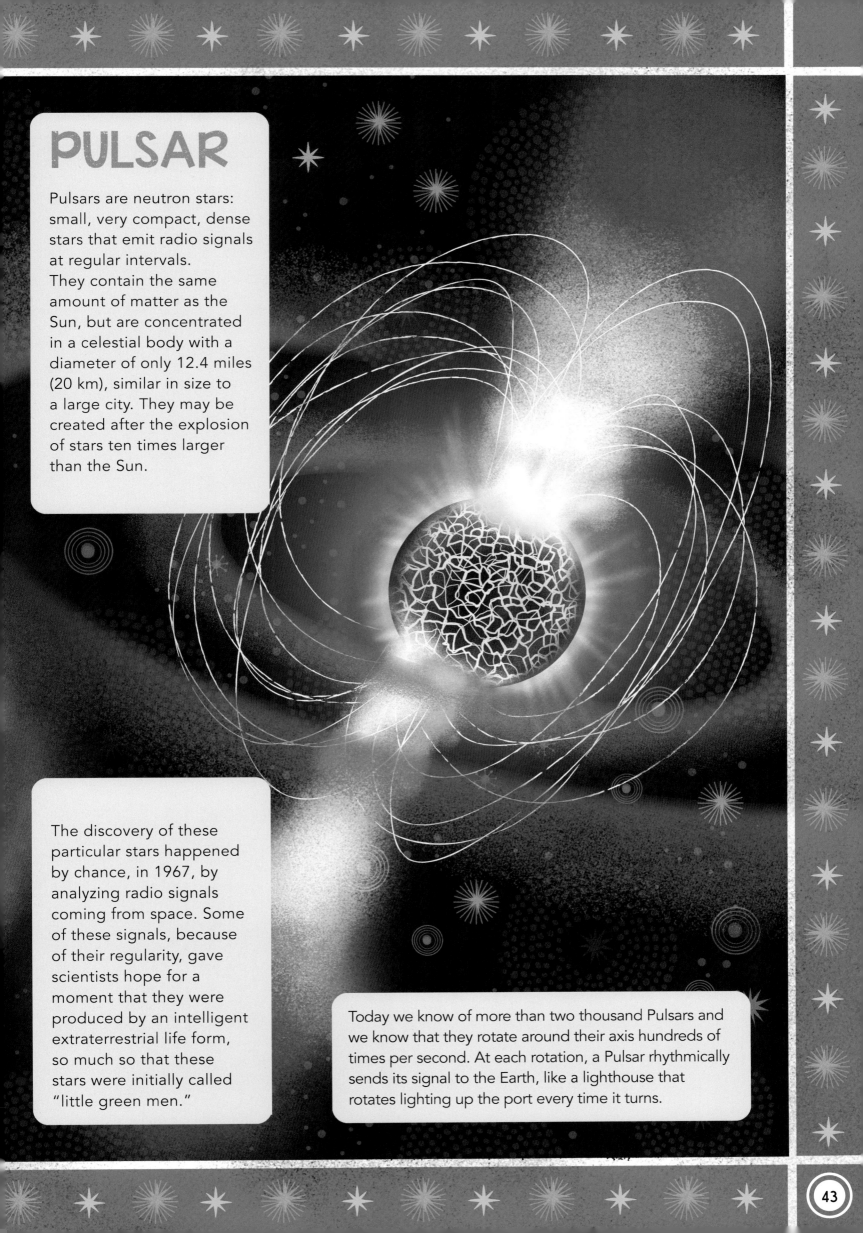

PULSAR

Pulsars are neutron stars: small, very compact, dense stars that emit radio signals at regular intervals. They contain the same amount of matter as the Sun, but are concentrated in a celestial body with a diameter of only 12.4 miles (20 km), similar in size to a large city. They may be created after the explosion of stars ten times larger than the Sun.

The discovery of these particular stars happened by chance, in 1967, by analyzing radio signals coming from space. Some of these signals, because of their regularity, gave scientists hope for a moment that they were produced by an intelligent extraterrestrial life form, so much so that these stars were initially called "little green men."

Today we know of more than two thousand Pulsars and we know that they rotate around their axis hundreds of times per second. At each rotation, a Pulsar rhythmically sends its signal to the Earth, like a lighthouse that rotates lighting up the port every time it turns.

QUASAR

Quasars (QUASi-stellAR radio sources) are very luminous celestial objects, emitting powerful radio waves and appearing on telescopes as dots similar to stars. In reality, Quasars are the nuclei of galaxies very far from the Earth (billions of light years) which emit large amounts of energy from their central area.

These celestial bodies were discovered in the 1960s, but it was not possible then to precisely identify their position. It was only in 1963 that scientists discovered that these objects were located outside our galaxy (the Milky Way) and with increasingly powerful telescopes, hundreds of thousands of Quasars were identified.

In the nucleus of these galaxies, there is a gigantic black hole, a celestial object with a force of gravity that is so strong that nothing can escape it. Its name derives from this very characteristic: whatever comes close to it falls into it without being able to get out of it. Even light! A black hole behaves, therefore, like a gigantic space funnel!

When dust, gas or even entire stars are attracted to black holes, before crossing the edge of this space funnel, they reach temperatures of millions of degrees and emit light.
This is why Quasars are very bright and can shine like 40,000 billion stars similar to our Sun.

Despite their brightness, Quasars are very difficult to observe due to their enormous distance from Earth. The farthest away, discovered in 2017, is 13 billion light years away from us: this means that today we see the light that started from the Quasar 13 billion years ago. Its radiation, therefore, was emitted when the Universe, which is 13.8 billion years old, had just been born.

This Quasar is, therefore, a "photograph" of what happened shortly after the Big Bang and studying it will help us to understand how they originated and how galaxies evolved! Astronomers think that there are other Quasars as old as this one and, therefore, they have not stopped looking up to the sky for their research.

r

ROSETTA

Rosetta is a probe that was launched in March 2004 by the European Space Agency and which landed only in August 2014! After ten years of travel, it reached its destination: the Comet 67P / Churyumov-Gerasimenko.
The mission ended on September 30, 2016, when the probe crashed on the comet, finally turning off!

The mission was made up of the Rosetta probe, which orbited the comet and accompanied it on its journey to the Sun, and a vehicle, Philae, which landed on Comet 67P on November 12, 2016. The aim was to study the origin of the comets to better understand the birth of the Solar System.

The names were not chosen at random. In fact, just as the Rosetta stone (the stone slab that shows ancient inscriptions in three different languages) and the obelisk found on the island of Philae have allowed researchers to decipher Egyptian hieroglyphics, so astronomers hoped that this mission would lead to "deciphering" the mysteries of the Solar System.

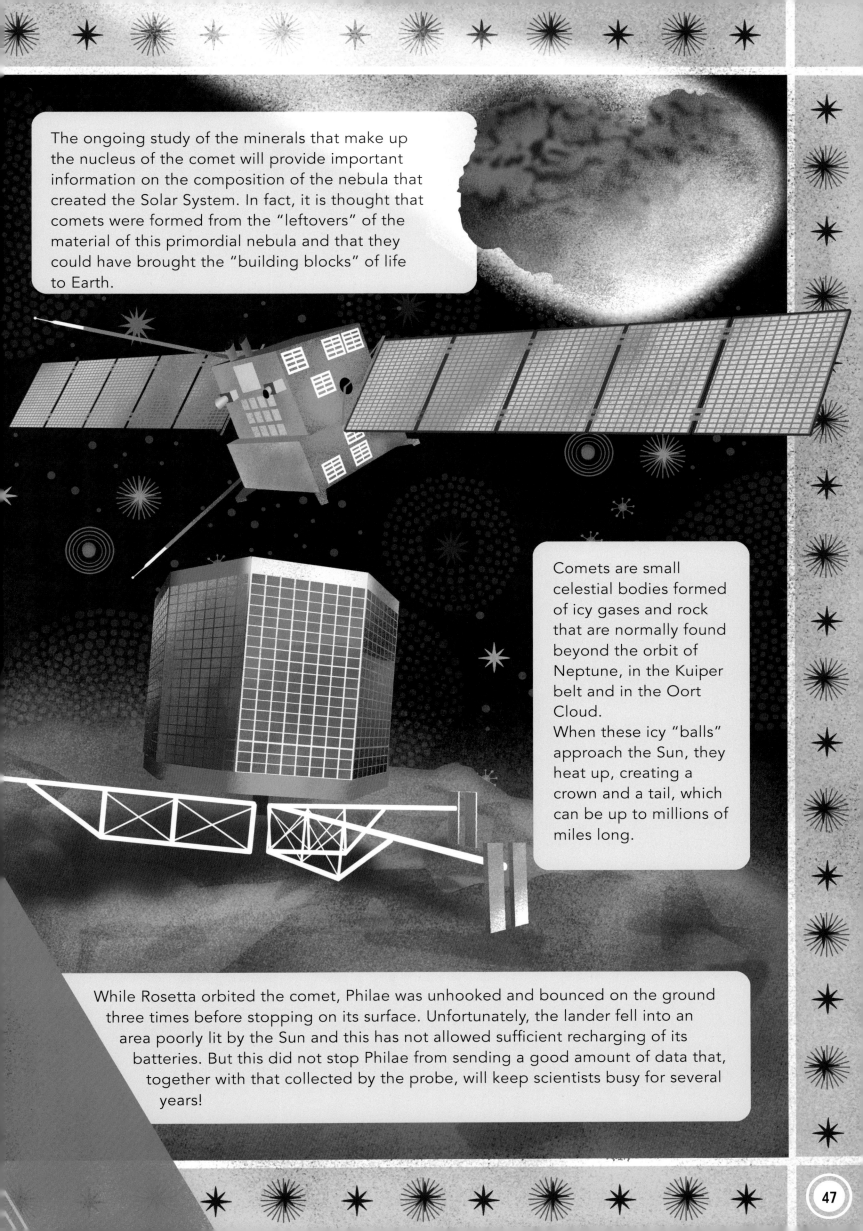

The ongoing study of the minerals that make up the nucleus of the comet will provide important information on the composition of the nebula that created the Solar System. In fact, it is thought that comets were formed from the "leftovers" of the material of this primordial nebula and that they could have brought the "building blocks" of life to Earth.

Comets are small celestial bodies formed of icy gases and rock that are normally found beyond the orbit of Neptune, in the Kuiper belt and in the Oort Cloud.
When these icy "balls" approach the Sun, they heat up, creating a crown and a tail, which can be up to millions of miles long.

While Rosetta orbited the comet, Philae was unhooked and bounced on the ground three times before stopping on its surface. Unfortunately, the lander fell into an area poorly lit by the Sun and this has not allowed sufficient recharging of its batteries. But this did not stop Philae from sending a good amount of data that, together with that collected by the probe, will keep scientists busy for several years!

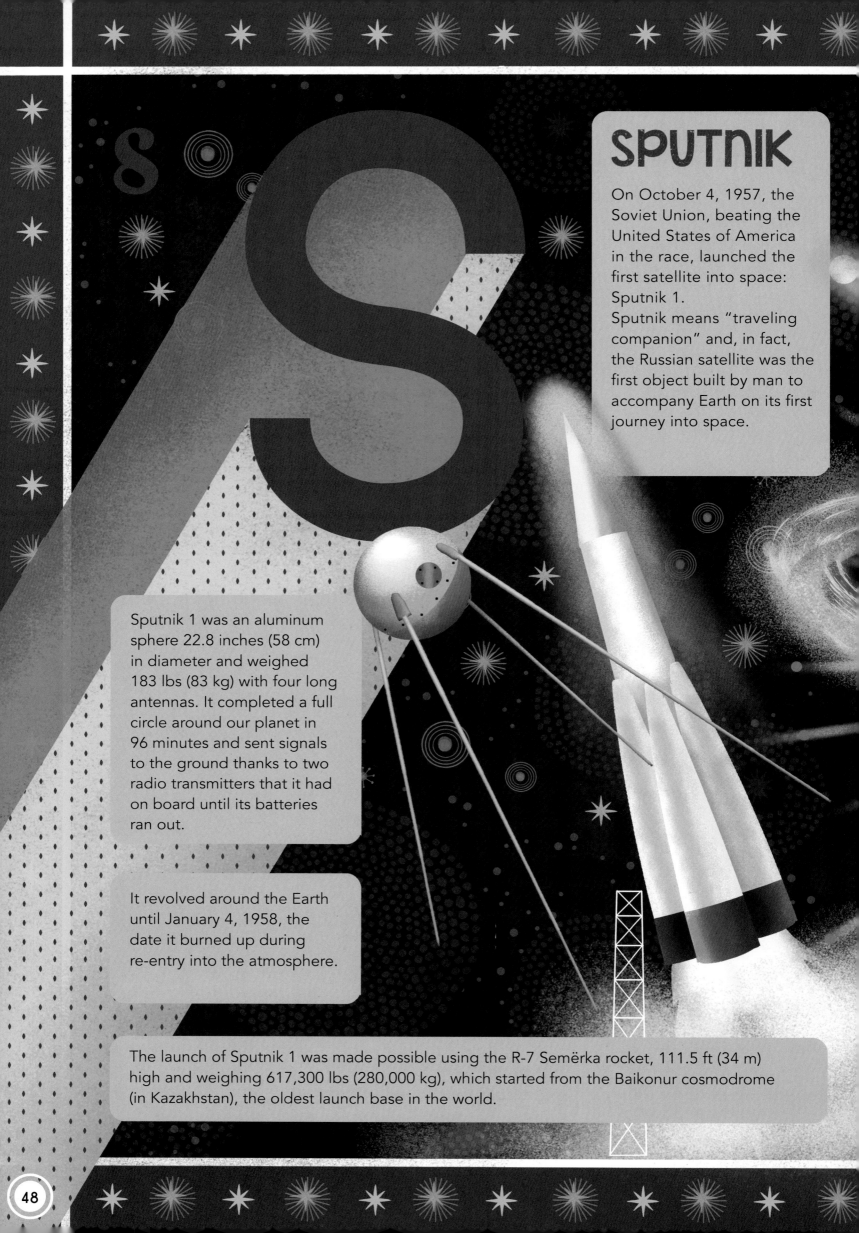

SPUTNIK

On October 4, 1957, the Soviet Union, beating the United States of America in the race, launched the first satellite into space: Sputnik 1.
Sputnik means "traveling companion" and, in fact, the Russian satellite was the first object built by man to accompany Earth on its first journey into space.

Sputnik 1 was an aluminum sphere 22.8 inches (58 cm) in diameter and weighed 183 lbs (83 kg) with four long antennas. It completed a full circle around our planet in 96 minutes and sent signals to the ground thanks to two radio transmitters that it had on board until its batteries ran out.

It revolved around the Earth until January 4, 1958, the date it burned up during re-entry into the atmosphere.

The launch of Sputnik 1 was made possible using the R-7 Semërka rocket, 111.5 ft (34 m) high and weighing 617,300 lbs (280,000 kg), which started from the Baikonur cosmodrome (in Kazakhstan), the oldest launch base in the world.

SUPERNOVA

A supernova is the explosion of a star that has reached the final stage of its existence. Suddenly and for a short time, the star becomes so bright that it can be seen from one galaxy to another.

The name derives from the Latin word *nova* which means "new" because it truly seems that a new start appears in the sky following the explosion. It is also called super to distinguish it from normal stellar explosions which are much less bright. In order for a supernova to occur, the mass of the star must be eight times larger than our Sun.

The oldest supernova observed from Earth was described by Chinese astronomers in 185 AD and it was visible in the sky for about eight months. The brightest one dates back to the year 1006. It appeared between April 30 and May 1 and was so bright that it could be observed even during the day.

In our galaxy, it is very difficult to see a supernova because of the presence of the dust that it hides: the last sighting dates back to October 9, 1604.

TEREŠKOVA

Valentina Tereškova was the first woman to be launched into space in 1963 aboard the Vostok 6 capsule, she made 49 orbits around our planet. Valentina worked as a designer, was a paratrooper expert and had a passion for space, so much so that she participated in and passed the exam to become a cosmonaut, together with four other companions.

She was the only one of this group of women to actually fly in space. To see another female Russian cosmonaut, the world would have to wait until 1982, when Svletana Savitzakaia was launched aboard the Soyuz capsule and became the first woman to take a space "walk" which lasted about three and a half hours!

NASA, unlike the Russian Space Agency, did not select a woman for space missions until 1983, when Sally Ride flew aboard the Space Shuttle. In 1961, thirteen women passed the first tests to become astronauts, but the program was canceled before the last medical visits and the American women never flew!

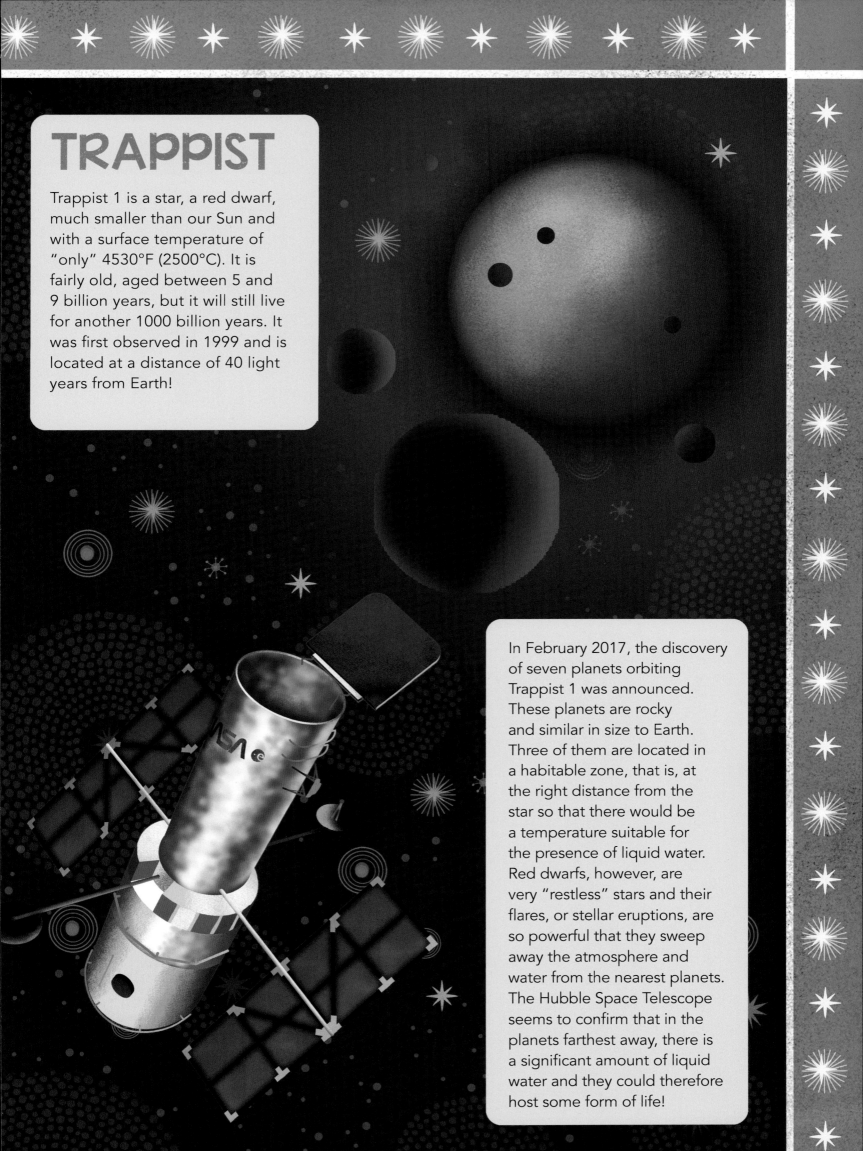

TRAPPIST

Trappist 1 is a star, a red dwarf, much smaller than our Sun and with a surface temperature of "only" 4530°F (2500°C). It is fairly old, aged between 5 and 9 billion years, but it will still live for another 1000 billion years. It was first observed in 1999 and is located at a distance of 40 light years from Earth!

In February 2017, the discovery of seven planets orbiting Trappist 1 was announced. These planets are rocky and similar in size to Earth. Three of them are located in a habitable zone, that is, at the right distance from the star so that there would be a temperature suitable for the presence of liquid water. Red dwarfs, however, are very "restless" stars and their flares, or stellar eruptions, are so powerful that they sweep away the atmosphere and water from the nearest planets. The Hubble Space Telescope seems to confirm that in the planets farthest away, there is a significant amount of liquid water and they could therefore host some form of life!

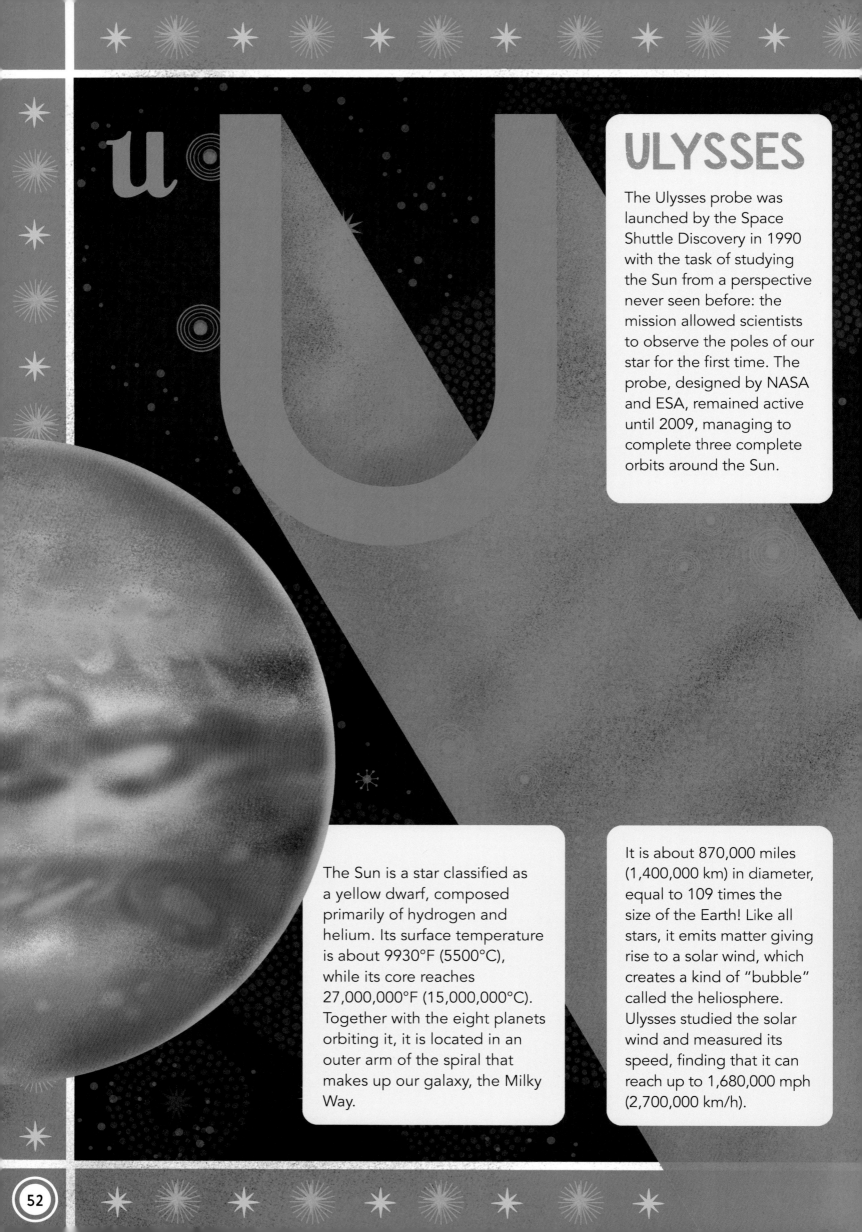

ULYSSES

The Ulysses probe was launched by the Space Shuttle Discovery in 1990 with the task of studying the Sun from a perspective never seen before: the mission allowed scientists to observe the poles of our star for the first time. The probe, designed by NASA and ESA, remained active until 2009, managing to complete three complete orbits around the Sun.

The Sun is a star classified as a yellow dwarf, composed primarily of hydrogen and helium. Its surface temperature is about 9930°F (5500°C), while its core reaches 27,000,000°F (15,000,000°C). Together with the eight planets orbiting it, it is located in an outer arm of the spiral that makes up our galaxy, the Milky Way.

It is about 870,000 miles (1,400,000 km) in diameter, equal to 109 times the size of the Earth! Like all stars, it emits matter giving rise to a solar wind, which creates a kind of "bubble" called the heliosphere. Ulysses studied the solar wind and measured its speed, finding that it can reach up to 1,680,000 mph (2,700,000 km/h).

The probe, before approaching the Sun, flew over Jupiter in February 1992, at a distance of about 250,000 miles (400,000 km). During its passage, it picked up a radio signal from the south pole of the gas giant, which was repeated every 40 minutes for a few hours. The same signal was then also detected at the north pole and seems to be connected to the interaction of the solar wind with the magnetic field of the planet.

Ulysses also passed three times through the material coming from the tail of a comet: the first time in May 1996, when it met the comet Hyakutake. Its tail was 310 million miles (half a billion km) long, more than three times the distance between the Earth and the Sun. The probe showed, therefore, that tails of comets are much longer than what was believed!

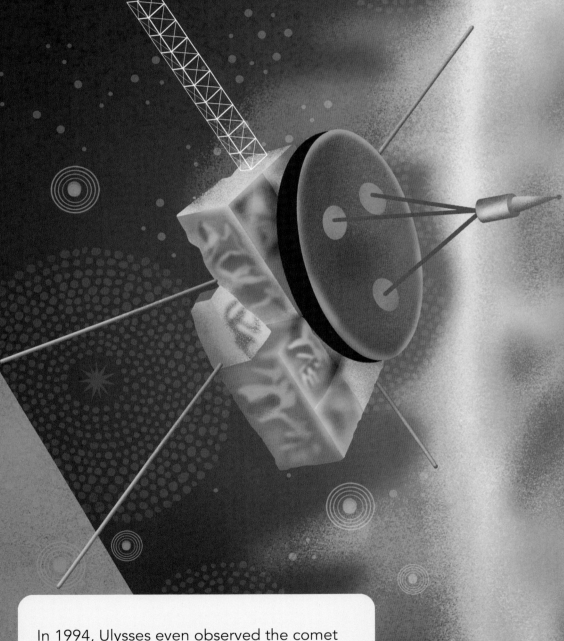

In 1994, Ulysses even observed the comet Shoemaker-Levy 9 on Jupiter! The comet, discovered in 1993, was the first that orbited around a planet and not around the Sun. This was the first time that a comet fell on a planet.

VEGGIE

In May 2014, the Veggie project began.
It was the first plant cultivation on board the International Space Station. After thirty-three days of treatment by astronaut Steve Swanson, the first spatial salad was collected, though it was not eaten on board but sent to Earth to be analyzed in the laboratory!

Just over a year later, other seeds were planted and, after 33 days, the fruits were harvested: on August 10, 2015, the Expedition 44 astronauts were able to eat lettuce grown in space for the first time! The first space flower also blossomed in 2016: astronaut Scott Kelly managed to create a real garden!

The success of the Veggie experiment is very important for preparing future long-term missions, such as a mankind's possible journey to Mars! Growing vegetables on board the space capsules would allow the astronauts to be autonomous, being able to consume fresh food and reducing the amount of supplies needed for the trip!

VOYAGER

On September 5, 1977, NASA launched the Voyager 1 spacecraft with the mission to fly over Jupiter, Saturn and its satellite Titan. After carrying out its tasks, the probe continued its space travel and in 2012, it reached the boundaries of the Solar System, entering interstellar space.

This probe represents the object built by man that today is farthest from the Earth and continues to work thanks to powerful plutonium battery cells. Voyager 1 and its twin Voyager 2 have photographed the rings of Jupiter and on its satellite, Io, have discovered the first volcanoes located off of Earth.

On November 28, 2017, after 37 long years, NASA rekindled the engines of the probe, which is 21 billion kilometers from Earth, to change its trajectory! After 19 hours and 35 minutes, the signal arrived that the maneuver had been successful. The Voyager can thus continue to communicate with our planet until at least 2025, when the instruments on board will no longer receive enough energy to operate.

WR

The WR stars, or stars of Wolf-Rayet, are named after the two French astronomers who discovered them in 1867. They are stars that, at birth, have a large mass, at least 20 times that of our Sun. During their life, however, due to the powerful stellar winds, they lose an enormous amount of matter from the outermost areas, leaving the hot core uncovered.

This is this reason why the surface temperature of WR stars is very high, between 54,000 and 360,000°F (30,000 and 200,000°C), and they are millions more times bright than the Sun. Because they have an intense period of activity, they burn their fuel quickly and explode in a supernova: their life, therefore, is very short.

When they reach the end of their existence, the temperature increases greatly and they generate powerful stellar winds that reach a speed of up to five and a half million miles per hour. The material expelled from the star forms a nebula that could then give rise to new stars and planets!

The brightest and most visible to Earth is Gamma Velorum, a WR star accompanied by a blue supergiant. This star is found in the constellation of the Sails. Today, its mass is "only" nine times that of the Sun, but at the beginning it was over 35 times larger than the Sun.

The Hubble Space Telescope has revealed that most WR stars have a companion star that orbits them, just like the first three WRs that were discovered!
In our galaxy, the Milky Way, about 500 WR stars have been identified, but many others are scattered in the galaxies around us!

Despite the fact that WR stars have an impressive mass, they are not the largest stars known today. In the Large Magellanic Cloud, at a distance of 165,000 light years from Earth, we can find the star R136a1 which makes even WR stars appear "tiny": its mass is 265 times that of the Sun and it is nine million times brighter!

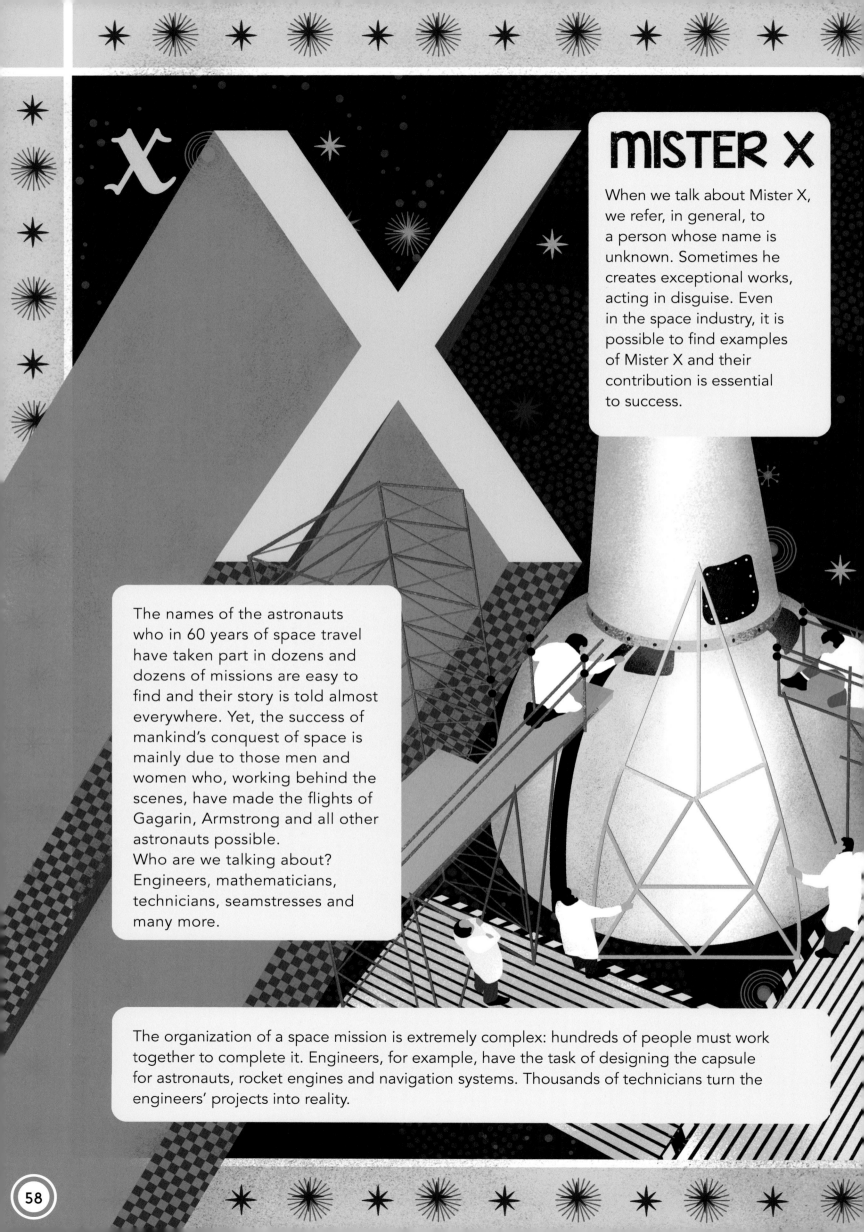

X

MISTER X

When we talk about Mister X, we refer, in general, to a person whose name is unknown. Sometimes he creates exceptional works, acting in disguise. Even in the space industry, it is possible to find examples of Mister X and their contribution is essential to success.

The names of the astronauts who in 60 years of space travel have taken part in dozens and dozens of missions are easy to find and their story is told almost everywhere. Yet, the success of mankind's conquest of space is mainly due to those men and women who, working behind the scenes, have made the flights of Gagarin, Armstrong and all other astronauts possible.
Who are we talking about?
Engineers, mathematicians, technicians, seamstresses and many more.

The organization of a space mission is extremely complex: hundreds of people must work together to complete it. Engineers, for example, have the task of designing the capsule for astronauts, rocket engines and navigation systems. Thousands of technicians turn the engineers' projects into reality.

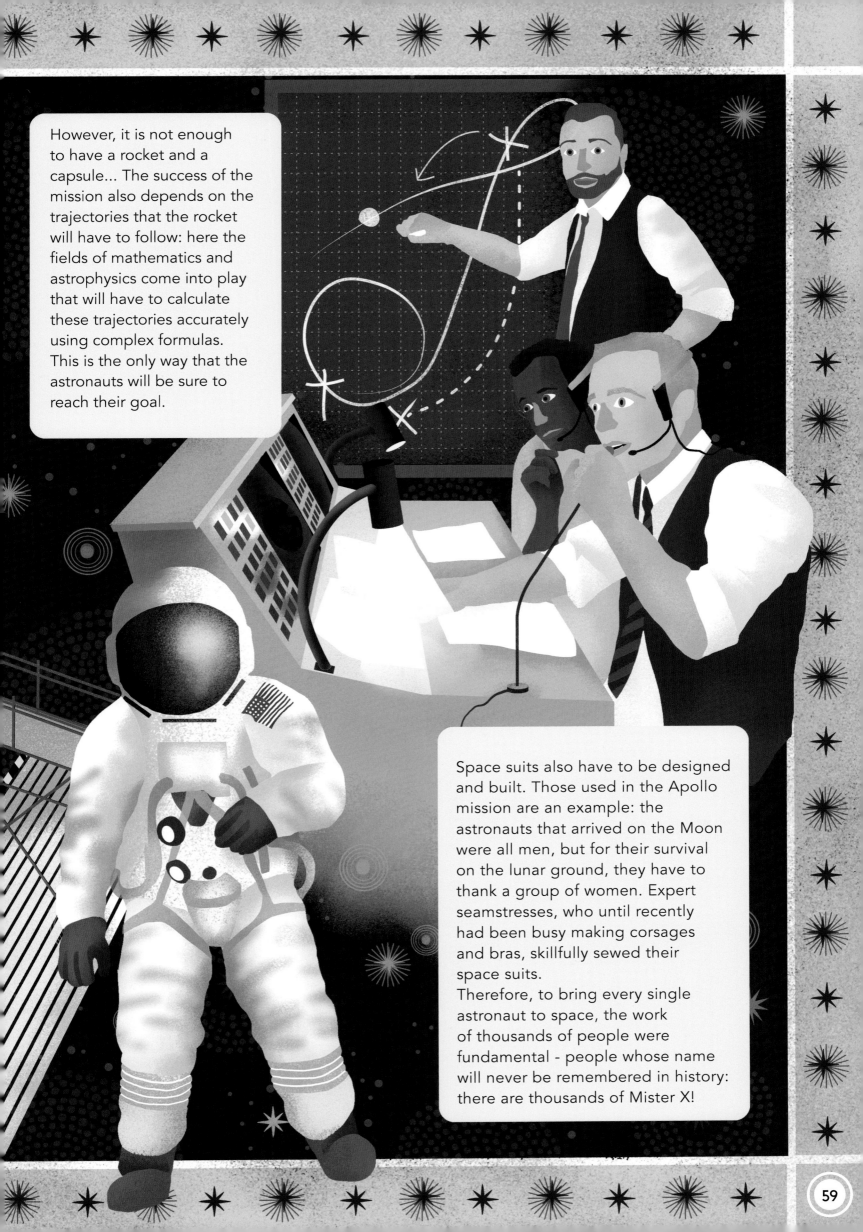

However, it is not enough to have a rocket and a capsule... The success of the mission also depends on the trajectories that the rocket will have to follow: here the fields of mathematics and astrophysics come into play that will have to calculate these trajectories accurately using complex formulas. This is the only way that the astronauts will be sure to reach their goal.

Space suits also have to be designed and built. Those used in the Apollo mission are an example: the astronauts that arrived on the Moon were all men, but for their survival on the lunar ground, they have to thank a group of women. Expert seamstresses, who until recently had been busy making corsages and bras, skillfully sewed their space suits.
Therefore, to bring every single astronaut to space, the work of thousands of people were fundamental - people whose name will never be remembered in history: there are thousands of Mister X!

YOUNG

John Young, born in San Francisco in 1930, was an American astronaut, the only one to have flown with three different space projects: Gemini, Apollo and STS (better known as the Space Shuttle)! He has been to space six times: the first as a pilot of the Gemini 3 capsule on March 23, 1965, and the last as commander of the STS-9 mission, almost twenty years later, on December 8, 1983.

Young joined the group of NASA astronauts in 1962 when the Gemini project started, so-called because for the first time the capsule could bring two men into space. Until then, the Mercury spacecraft had been launched with only one astronaut on board. Together with his commander, Virgil Grissom, Young obtained the distinction of taking part in the first American space flight in pairs.

Thanks to the Gemini program, in which Young used the first computer in space, the Apollo program was subsequently developed which in 1969 brought mankind to the Moon. Young also played an important role in this program: he belonged to the crew of Apollo 10, the mission known as the "general rehearsal for the Moon."

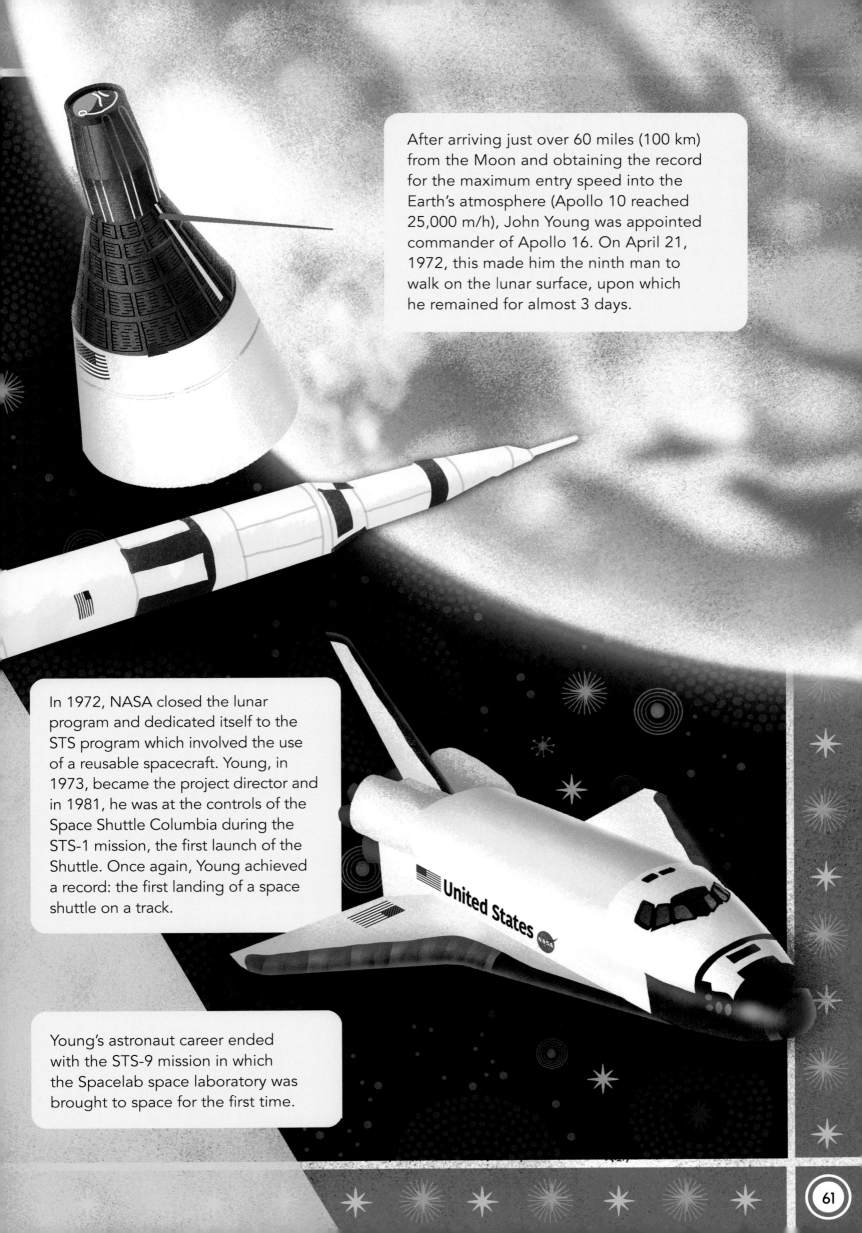

After arriving just over 60 miles (100 km) from the Moon and obtaining the record for the maximum entry speed into the Earth's atmosphere (Apollo 10 reached 25,000 m/h), John Young was appointed commander of Apollo 16. On April 21, 1972, this made him the ninth man to walk on the lunar surface, upon which he remained for almost 3 days.

In 1972, NASA closed the lunar program and dedicated itself to the STS program which involved the use of a reusable spacecraft. Young, in 1973, became the project director and in 1981, he was at the controls of the Space Shuttle Columbia during the STS-1 mission, the first launch of the Shuttle. Once again, Young achieved a record: the first landing of a space shuttle on a track.

Young's astronaut career ended with the STS-9 mission in which the Spacelab space laboratory was brought to space for the first time.

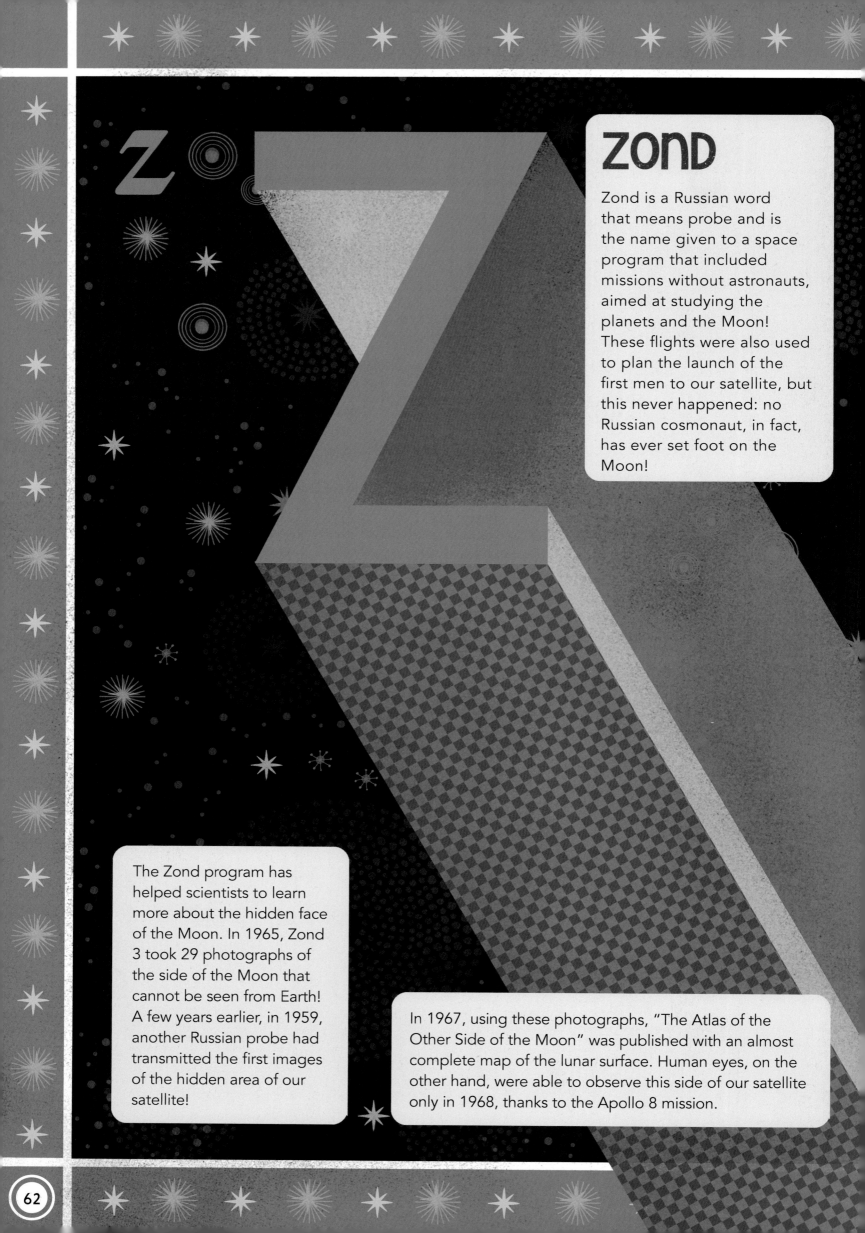

ZOND

Zond is a Russian word that means probe and is the name given to a space program that included missions without astronauts, aimed at studying the planets and the Moon! These flights were also used to plan the launch of the first men to our satellite, but this never happened: no Russian cosmonaut, in fact, has ever set foot on the Moon!

The Zond program has helped scientists to learn more about the hidden face of the Moon. In 1965, Zond 3 took 29 photographs of the side of the Moon that cannot be seen from Earth! A few years earlier, in 1959, another Russian probe had transmitted the first images of the hidden area of our satellite!

In 1967, using these photographs, "The Atlas of the Other Side of the Moon" was published with an almost complete map of the lunar surface. Human eyes, on the other hand, were able to observe this side of our satellite only in 1968, thanks to the Apollo 8 mission.

When we pass "behind" the Moon, all radio communications with Earth are interrupted. For this reason, no vehicle has ever landed on its hidden side! It was only in 2007 that the Japanese Space Agency, using the Kaguya probe, brought a satellite into the lunar orbit to keep telecommunications open!

In 1968, Zond 5 was the first probe to perform a flight over the Moon and return to Earth "healthy and safe" with its cargo consisting of turtles, flies, plants, seeds and bacteria.
This mission showed that living beings could survive a trip around the Moon! The turtles had lost 10% of their mass but had not suffered any particular damage!

After the closure of the Zond program, probes of subsequent missions have also brought back samples of lunar rocks to Earth. In 1970, the first of three robotic missions was launched which, after collecting samples, drilled into the soil with a drill and gathered 3.5 oz (101 g) of it which were then sent to Earth. After three days of travel, the capsule landed in Kazakhstan with its precious cargo!

ANNALISA BEGHELLI

She graduated in Architecture in Venice in 2006, but after 4 years of working experience chose to follow her passion for drawing and make it her new profession. In 2011, she specialized in illustration and editorial design at MiMaster in Milan, where she currently lives. She works as a freelance illustrator and in 2017, founded FAI 31, a brand with which she develops communication projects of a training nature, based on the use of editorial tools, able to make people talk about themselves in a transversal, innovative way.

DIEGO MATTARELLI

He graduated in Geological Sciences and Technologies from the University of Milan – Bicocca and deals with the scientific dissemination at various levels, for schools of all levels and for the general public, collaborating with various institutions and museums. He gained experience in scholastic publishing as the co-author of a middle school science course as well as in the publishing of popular science. Since 2005, he has been working as an explainer at the Museum of Natural History in Milan and several other scientific exhibitions, some of which he has also helped to create.

EMANUELA PAGLIARI

She graduated in Natural Sciences at the University of Milan and has been working as an explainer for several years at the Museum of Natural History in Milan and for several other scientific exhibitions. She collaborates in the creation of recreational-educational material for schools and the general public. She has acquired editorial experience in the field of scholastics and is the co-author of a middle school science course.

© 2018 White Star s.r.l.

First Racehorse for Young Readers Edition 2020

Racehorse Publishing books may be purchased in bulk at special discounts for sales promotion, corporate gifts, fund-raising, or educational purposes. Special editions can also be created to specifications. For details, contact the Special Sales Department, Skyhorse Publishing, 307 West 36th Street, 11th Floor, New York, NY 10018 or info@skyhorsepublishing.com.

Racehorse Publishing™ and Racehorse for Young Readers™ are registered trademarks of Skyhorse Publishing, Inc.®, a Delaware corporation.

Visit our website at www.skyhorsepublishing.com.

10 9 8 7 6 5 4 3 2 1

Library of Congress Cataloging-in-Publication Data is available on file.

Translation and Editing: TperTradurre srl, Rome

Print ISBN: 978-1-63158-591-3
E-Book ISBN: 978-1-63158-592-0

Printed in China